THE LOSS OF THE *CRICCIETH CASTLE*

The Loss Of The *Criccieth Castle*

by Cathy Woodhead

ISBN: 978-0-9561469-1-5

Published in 2012 by Delfryn Publications, Delfryn, Borth-y-Gest, Porthmadog, Gwynedd LL49 9TW, UK
Telephone: +44 (0)1766 512115
Website: www.delfrynpublications.co.uk

The title page shows one of the Falkland Islands postage stamps released to commemorate ships known as the 'Cape Horners'. The stamp with the *Criccieth Castle* had a value of £1.

Cover designed by Cathy Woodhead from a painting of the *Criccieth Castle* by Robert D Cadwalader

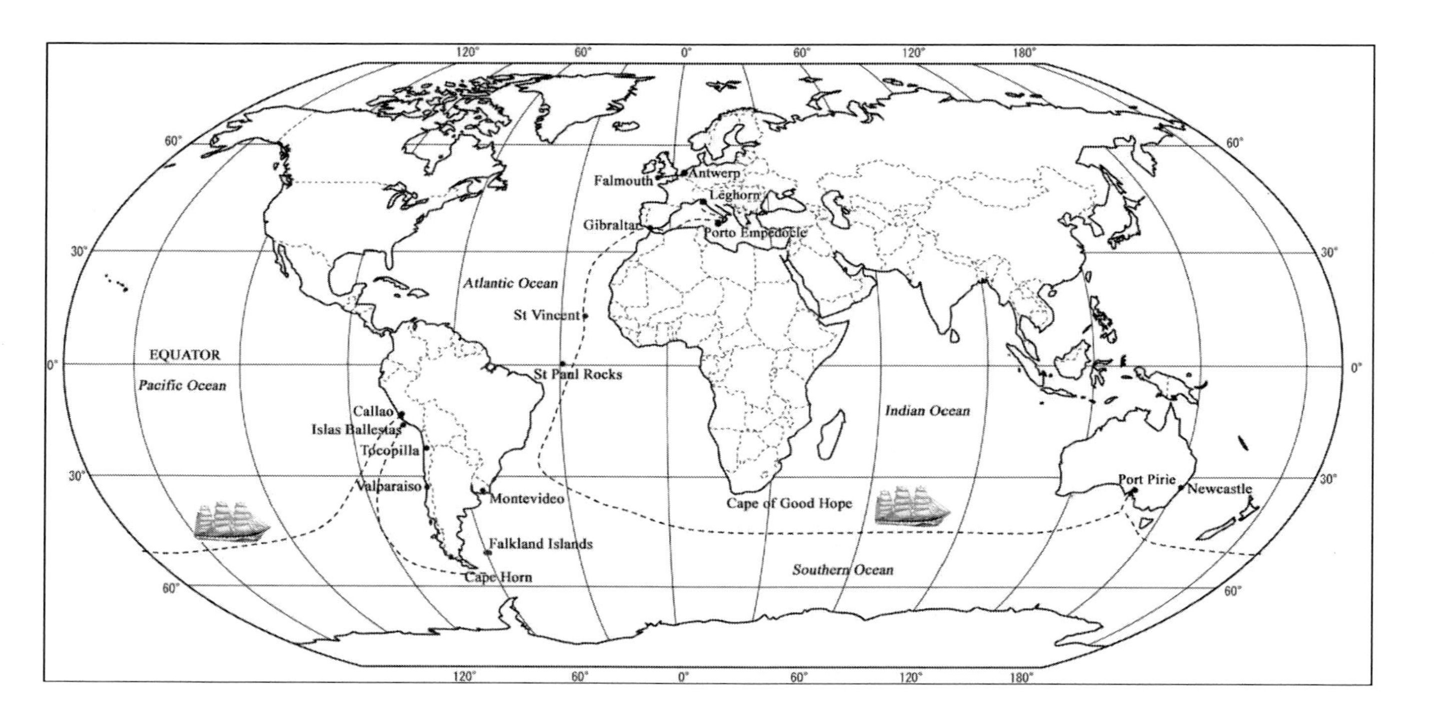

The 1911 to 1912 voyage of the Criccieth Castle

CONTENTS

FOREWORD

by Robert D Cadwalader

I first heard this story as I was growing up in the small Welsh town of Criccieth; the very place whose ancient castle the ship in this book is named after. Nowadays it is a pleasant holiday resort but in the past it was a hive of maritime activity. Large square rigged ships were owned and managed here, crewed by local men. There were dozens of Master Mariners, mates, stewards and sailors. These men often started their seagoing careers as ship's boys on the schooners and brigs sailing out of nearby Porthmadog in the coastal and Atlantic trade then moved on to the larger deep-sea ships sailing out of Liverpool and the South Wales ports to Australia and the West Coast of South America.

These were long trips sometimes the men would be away for up to two years. Communication was poor and perhaps a letter would take months to arrive. The mothers and wives back in Criccieth ran the homes and worried about their sons and husbands, for the seafarer's life was fraught with perils and there are several gravestones in the cemetery inscribed 'lost at sea' or 'died of fever'.

Most of the shipowners allowed the Master to have their wives accompany them on these voyages and many did. While they did not have to work the ships as the men did they still had to endure the months at sea, terrible weather, sickness and bad food. They supported their husbands and provided a softer, female touch to the rough male world of the ship.

There are many untold tales of the hardships these women suffered. Many gave birth while at sea, perhaps in the middle of a gale rounding Cape Horn. Several were lost with their husbands and the whole crew when the ship foundered. Some were shipwrecked.

It is good that this story is being told before it slips from memory. Cathy Woodhead has used her mother's transcription and all existing accounts supplemented by thorough research into the crew agreements, wreck inquiry reports and newspaper articles. It vividly portrays the hardships and suffering that Catherine Thomas and the crew of the *Criccieth Castle* went through when her husband's ship foundered off Cape Horn a hundred years ago.

Robert Dafydd Cadwalader
Mariner and Artist
Y Stiwdio
Criccieth

A Criccieth boy dreams of going to sea (R D Cadwalader)

PREFACE

In 2009 I found a typed copy of a story called 'The Wreck of the Criccieth Castle' in my mother's papers. It began with this introduction: 'This is a tale told by one of the most recent members to join the British Section of the Cape Horners, Catherine Thomas. She is the widow of Captain Robert Thomas who in 1912 was master of the *Criccieth Castle* on the voyage around Cape Horn which proved to be her last. This narrative describes how in mid-winter in the stormiest region of the world the captain, his wife Catherine and their four-year-old son, were forced with all the crew to abandon the vessel and take to the boats. What followed was a fight for their lives. Stories such as this, stories of long-continued hardship and dogged endurance, are rare in these days of fast ships and radio communication.'

Attached to the manuscript was a letter dated 14th April 1958 from Catherine Thomas to my mother, Jocelyn Greenway. The story fired my imagination to such an extent that I set out to find out as much as I could about the Thomas family and all the circumstances surrounding the story. This book is the result.

In August 1957 Commander Claude Woollard, a retired Royal Navy officer who lived in Poole, Dorset founded the British Section of the International Association of Cape Horners (IACH) – for those who have voyaged around Cape Horn under sail. Woollard ran the training ship *English Rose II* and through his training cruises he made strong links with St Malo and the Association there. Catherine Thomas contacted Commander Woollard about the IACH when it was first set up in Britain. When Woollard heard Catherine's story he wanted to include it in his book 'The Last of The Cape Horners' and for this he needed the services of a journalist to write the story. In the previous year my mother, a freelance journalist, had written an article about Woollard's ship called 'Aboard a Girls' Training Ship' and in 1958 another article called 'Cape Horn Sailors Get Together' about the founding of the IACH British Section. (These two articles are in Appendix III of this book.) Woollard now asked Jocelyn if she would be interested in writing up Catherine Thomas' story using an account that her husband Captain Thomas had written for The Wide World Magazine in 1913.

Jocelyn rewrote the story using Catherine's perspective and sent a draft typed copy to Catherine for approval. In April 1958 Catherine replied to Jocelyn with the draft attached. It was this and Catherine's reply that I had found in my mother's box of papers. In the letter Catherine wrote:

'Dear Mrs Greenway

First of all please pardon my delay in answering your kind letter and also the draft of 'The Wreck of the Criccieth Castle'. It is awfully kind of you and Commander Woollard to go to all this trouble. I can't improve on it. It is extremely good the way you have done it. I really feel very grateful to you. I am very glad that the Cape Horners' Association is progressing so well. I understand that Commander Woollard is the founder of the British Section and has done a lot for it. I had lost interest in the Sea until I saw about the 'Cape Horners'. I understand that they have their 14th Annual Congress of the International Association at St Malo. I have not yet decided whether I shall go or not. We've had a hard winter; as you say the weather is improving and a little Spring sunshine will help to cheer us up. Again accept my most grateful thanks for your kind interest. Kind regards. Yours sincerely Catherine Thomas.'

Jocelyn's chapter subsequently appeared in Woollard's book, although Jocelyn is not mentioned as it credits the chapter, understandably, to Catherine.

A few years later in 1963 a journalist called Jane Deverson must have met and interviewed Catherine Thomas as she wrote an article for Woman's Own magazine called 'I Married The Sea' which appeared on March 16th 1963. This article provided details of how and when Catherine met Robert as well as conversations and details that I have incorporated into this account.

Investigating the story soon led me to Robert Cadwalader's very helpful website (see Appendix II) which amongst other things details the ships and shipping companies from North Wales and in particular from Criccieth. Catherine's granddaughter, Sylvia Swainson, had also found Robert's website and through Robert I was able to get in touch with her. At about this time Sylvia had realised a lifelong ambition to visit the Falkland Islands and see for herself where the lifeboat had landed on the island. Sylvia kindly shared everything she had on the story with me. This included a copy of Robert's 1913 article in The Wide World Magazine, the Woman's Own article from 1963, various newspaper cuttings from The Falkland Islands Magazine and Church Paper and some old photographs, all of which were a great help in piecing the story together. My thanks go to Greg Ray, an avid collector of The Wide World Magazine, who provided me with the scans of the pictures from the 1913 magazine. These pictures are indicated in the captions by 'WWM 1913'.

My own research led me to the report of the 1912 Board of Trade Inquiry into the loss of the *Criccieth Castle*, and this is printed in full in Appendix VIII. I also discovered a very interesting article in a 1933 Sea Breezes magazine written by Edmund Howard, a crew member, from his 1908 to 1909 voyage in the *Criccieth Castle.* I found census returns and birth, marriage and death certificates, and many more newspaper articles, and I found out what became of Bobby, the four-year-old boy who survived the shipwreck. Robert Cadwalader has helped me a great deal and provided some of the illustrations for this book. It was through him that I learnt of the significance of the crew agreements and the wealth of information that they contain. Many crew agreements are held by the Archive Department of the University of Newfoundland which agreed to house these invaluable documents at a time when they were about to be discarded. See Appendix VII for more information about crew agreements and examples from the *Criccieth Castle*'s last voyage of 1911 to 1912.

In 2009 I contacted the television presenter, Trevor Fishlock, in the hope that he might be interested in making a programme about the story of the *Criccieth Castle.* Trevor was intrigued by the story and in 2011 his half-hour programme 'Mother Courage' was broadcast on ITV Wales.

Also in 2009 I submitted my mother's article about the *Criccieth Castle* to Cymru a'r Môr and it appeared in Maritime Wales 2009 Number 30 pp 46-54.

In 2010 I was lucky enough to discover the whereabouts of the family Bible that had belonged to Catherine's parents, William and Ellen Pritchard. The family tree from this appears in Appendix V. I found a copy of the Board of Trade Inquiry into the 1904 loss of the *Eivion,* during Robert Thomas' first command and this can be found in Appendix XV. Leona Roberts of the Falkland Islands Museum & National Trust and Jim Elliott have provided me with useful information and photographs from the Falkland Islands.

I would like to thank everyone who has helped by reading drafts of the book at its various stages. Questions from them led me to include a glossary of nautical terms and a bibliography in Appendices I and II.

I have used all these sources to provide the following account of a truly remarkable survival story. While doing this I could not help musing on the obvious comparison with Shackleton's epic voyages to Elephant Island and South Georgia, remembering that these men had volunteered for adventure and exploration, whilst Captain Thomas with his pregnant wife and child, and all the crew on board the *Criccieth Castle,* were not out for adventure – they were trying to earn a living. I also have thought about the countless people and ships that have been lost at sea over the years and whose stories have never been told.

CHWILOG
241.

GORSANEDD,
LLANGYBI,
CHWILOG,
CAERNARVONSHIRE.

14. 4. 58

Dear Mrs Greenway,
First of all please pardon my delay in answering your kind letter and also the draft of the "Wreck of the "Criccieth Castle".
It is awfully kind of you and Commander Woollard to go to all this trouble.
I can't improve on it; It is extremely good the way you have done it. I really feel very grateful to you.
I am very glad that

Catherine Thomas' letter to Jocelyn Greenway dated 14th April 1958

The "Cape Horners Association" is progressing so well.

I understand that "Commander Woolland" is the founder of the British Section and done a lot for it. I had lost interest in the Sea until I saw about the "Cape Horners".

I understand that they have their 14th annual Congress of the International Association at St Malo, I have not yet decided whether I shall go or not.

We've had a hard winter; as you say the weather is improving and a little Spring sunshine will help to cheer us up. Again accept my most grateful thanks for your kind interest. Kind regards.

Yours Sincerely

Catherine Thomas

Chapter 1

EARLY DAYS

From the lane outside her father's shop in Llangybi, the young Catherine Pritchard could see across the fields down to Tremadog Bay three miles away. She would watch the sailing vessels leaving Porthmadog to deliver slate to ports across the world. She longed to set sail with them and visit the faraway places she had read about in books.

The old post office and shop in Llangybi where Catherine grew up

Llangybi, where Catherine was born in 1885, is a village in the district of Eifionydd in what was then Caernarvonshire, now Gwynedd, in North Wales, six miles northwest of the coastal town and port of Pwllheli on the Llŷn peninsula. Catherine's father kept the local post office-cum-grocery and haberdashery shop which was also the family home. Catherine was the middle child of four brothers and two sisters, and the family led a happy community-based life centred on their home and the local chapel, Capel Helyg. Like the other girls in the neighbourhood, she could foresee the likely pattern of her life and she thought she would probably marry a local boy and settle down in the village.

The shipping industry dominated the lives of many families in the coastal towns. There were shipbuilders, sailmakers, carpenters, pilots, captains, crew and all manner of other related workers. But Catherine's family was not from a seafaring background. Her father William was the eleventh son of John Pritchard, a tailor in Llanfihangel Ysceifiog on Anglesey. Unlike her Welsh father, Catherine's mother was English. She was Ellen Evans and her father was a blacksmith in Liverpool. When Catherine's parents married on 3rd July 1874 in the Welsh Presbyterian Church, Toxteth Park, William was a commercial traveller. By 1881 William and Ellen with their growing family had moved to Llandwrog near Caernarfon where William was now a draper and tailor employing two men. Shortly after this the family moved to the property, Bryn Gwalia, in Llangybi – the post office and general store. Catherine's mother soon learnt to speak Welsh and this was the language of the family. When Catherine left school she trained to make hats and worked as a milliner in the nearby town of Pwllheli.

One day in 1905 when Catherine was 19 she met a man who would change her life forever, Robert Thomas, who had recently returned to North Wales after his ship the *Eivion* caught fire off Cape Horn.

Robert was from a seafaring family in Criccieth; both his father and grandfather were master mariners. Robert grew up knowing the dangers of a life at sea – in 1881 when he was only two years old his father, captain of the Porthmadog ship the

Cygnet, died from yellow fever in Rio Grande do Sul in South America and seven years later his cousin Charlie, a ship's boy only eight years older than Robert, was killed when he fell from the mast to the deck. Charlie was buried at Talcahuano in Chile. Despite these tragedies Robert was not discouraged and began his own nautical career at the early age of thirteen when he served on a Porthmadog schooner as a ship's boy. A year later in 1893 he became an apprentice on the *Criccieth Castle* managed by the firm of Messrs Robert Thomas (no relation) and Company of Criccieth and Liverpool. After later serving on the *Denbigh Castle* and the *Ednyfed* he was given command of the *Eivion* at the age of only 24 years.

Criccieth slipway in the late 1800s when Robert Thomas was a boy (R D Cadwalader)

Robert Thomas' first and only voyage with the *Eivion* was a memorable one. The *Eivion*, with a crew of 19 hands, left Garston, Liverpool on June 14th 1904 bound for Tocopilla in Chile with a cargo of Blundell's steam coal from the Lancashire collieries at Orrell. In early September they encountered a terrible storm off Cape Horn, which swept away all but one of the lifeboats, leaving them very vulnerable. Three weeks later they discovered that the cargo was on fire. Cases of spontaneous combustion of coal were not uncommon as it naturally reacts with oxygen resulting in a rise in temperature. When through poor ventilation this heat cannot escape, the temperature will continue to rise and the coal may catch fire.

On September 30th at 1600 the first mate noticed smoke was coming through the chain pipes forward, and on opening the forehatch cover he found the hold was full of smoke. He then noted that all three hatch covers were very hot. He ordered the crew to seal the holds completely, including the ventilators, to starve the coal of oxygen. However, at midnight on October 1st the forehatch covers were blown overboard by an explosion, no doubt caused by gases given off from the hot coal, and next morning at 0615 the afterhatch covers were also blown off. The ship hove-to and the excessive rolling of the ship which ensued caused the remaining lifeboat to break up at around 1500.

The situation was critical – the ship was on fire and there were no boats in which to escape. Then an hour later they had the good fortune to sight a vessel which proved to be the *Lonsdale* of Liverpool. They signalled with rockets, blue lights, and hoisted a flare-up light on the gaff-end of the mizzen mast. This was kept going until 2130 when the *Lonsdale* rounded the lee of the *Eivion* and promised to stand by until daylight. Wind and waves were increasing, the ship was rolling badly, and with each heavy roll more gases were released causing explosions that threw up large quantities of coals out of the holds.

As it became daylight it was clear that the *Eivion* was

beyond help and the crew needed to evacuate the ship as quickly as possible. At about 0630 the *Lonsdale* in a very heavy sea launched her lifeboat, manned by the first mate with four crew members.

The Eivion in Bristol Harbour (date unknown)

Through the night the wind had been blowing at gale force 8 (40 knots) and at daylight it increased to storm force 10 (50 knots). When the lifeboat came alongside the *Eivion*, a big sea crashed her against the ship, breaking some staves and partly filling her with water. Despite this, she returned to the *Lonsdale* with ten of the shipwrecked crew and then went back again to fetch the remaining nine – Captain Thomas and the two mates being the last to leave the ship. The *Eivion* was sinking with all hatch covers off and dense clouds of smoke rising from each hatch.

The *Lonsdale* brought the crew of the *Eivion* to Valparaiso. At the Naval Court of Inquiry held there in October it was found that Captain Robert Thomas had navigated his ship in a seamanlike and proper manner, doing everything in his power to save the ship and the lives of the crew. See Appendix XV for the Inquiry Report.

On his return to England Captain Fall of the *Lonsdale* was

presented with an inscribed silver bowl by the Lord Mayor of Liverpool, on behalf of the British Government, in recognition of what was described as 'the most outstanding deed of bravery of the year'. Sea Gallantry Medals were presented by the Board of Trade to the seamen from the *Lonsdale* who had so bravely manned the lifeboat: Mr J O'Connor, first mate; C Larsen, carpenter; J Read, sailmaker; M Morrisson, AB and F Gradike, AB.

After his ordeal Robert Thomas returned to his home in Criccieth to await his next appointment. One Sunday he happened to go to the chapel in Llangybi. Here he saw Catherine in the congregation and asked for an introduction. She was immediately taken with his strong-looking physique, dark hair, deep blue eyes and charming ways.

A few days after Robert met Catherine at the chapel, she was working at the milliner's when the shop door opened and Robert entered. Catherine, who had hardly stopped thinking about the handsome young captain, could not believe her luck when, after chatting, he invited her to go for a walk when she finished her work. For the next month they saw each other as often as possible, going for long walks along the sea front and in the countryside and talking, always in Welsh, about his life at sea and the many things they found they had in common having been raised in the same part of Wales. Amongst other places, they would undoubtedly have visited Ffynnon Gybi, a holy well in an idyllic location near Llangybi, from where they could climb up to the embankments of the Iron Age hill fort, Carn Bentyrch, lying on the hill above the well. From here they would have admired the breathtaking views along the Llŷn peninsula and across Cardigan Bay, talking of Robert's voyages across the oceans of the world.

When the time came for Robert to sail again Catherine had strong feelings for the handsome captain and she hoped more than anything that he felt the same way about her. Then the day before he left, to her joy, he asked her to marry him when he returned in two years' time from a voyage to Australia and South America and, of course, she agreed with alacrity! He was to take up his new post as the first mate of an iron-hulled sailing ship called the *Criccieth Castle*, a ship that Robert had served on as an apprentice in 1893 twelve years before.

The history of the ship prior to Robert's appointment is of interest. She was built and named the *Silverdale* by Williamsons of Workington in 1887 and two years later she was bought by Robert Thomas the shipowner who renamed her the *Criccieth Castle.* As was usual at that time a single ship company was set up, the Ship Criccieth Castle Company, and shares were sold. Initially it had its registered office in Criccieth but later moved to Liverpool. The 185 shares of £100 each in the new company were taken up within a matter of months by people in North Wales, in particular from the Llŷn peninsula. The 98 shareholders were an eclectic mix of wool merchants, accountants, surgeons, schoolmasters, school inspectors, ministers, widows and others. There are more details of the ship in Appendix VI.

The Criccieth Castle

The shipowner Robert Thomas, unrelated to Catherine's Robert, was a former Nefyn school teacher who became an entrepreneur, forming his own shipping companies. Through his skills he created investment opportunities for his shareholders on quite a grand scale, managing 30 ships at various times between 1878 and 1919. Not untypically for the shipping industry of the time, 18 of these 30 ships were lost at sea, sometimes, sadly, with loss of life. Many of his vessels were manned by local men and included the *Maelgwyn*, *Ednyfed* and *Penrhyn Castle* which were amongst the last of the great square-riggers. His ships traded worldwide carrying, for example, general cargo to Australia, coal and grain from Australia to the west coast of South America, nitrates from there to Europe, coal from Britain to steamship ports around the world and many others.

Sailing ships leaving European ports had to use the prevailing winds and ocean currents. They depended on the skills and experience of the captains and crew to find the quickest route to their destinations, and carried enough provisions to avoid stops at other ports on the way. Most voyages involved at least one rounding of Cape Horn – for sailors the most notorious place on earth with its storms and mountainous seas. Although the 'short way' to Australia through the Suez Canal had been opened for over 40 years, the tariffs and other costs involved did not warrant its use for sailing vessels. The cargos carried by sailing ships were non-perishable and of low value, so there was no urgency to get them to their destination. It was the ships' extremely low running costs that enabled these ships to continue in service for many years even while steamships grew in number. Sailing ships would carry European coal to many parts of the world for refuelling the steamers, which were unable to carry sufficient quantities of coal in addition to their cargos to make very long passages. The opening of the Panama Canal in 1914 was a nail in the coffin for the sailing fleet because it shortened the journey to the west coasts of South and North America.

Life on the sailing ships was very hard for everyone on

board. Often the food was poor and in short supply, the clothing was basic and the work extremely hard and dangerous. The crew had to climb the rigging to trim the sails in all weathers and if they fell then they would injure or kill themselves either by landing on the deck or in the sea, where rescue was virtually impossible due to the difficulties of stopping and manoeuvring a large sailing vessel. Wages for the crew were low being in the order of £2 a month for cabin boys and up to £7.10s a month for the first mate (this was equivalent to a miner's wage). Apprentices were not paid during their four years of training so it is not surprising that some voyages could have as many as nine apprentices on board at any one time. The margins between profit and loss were tight and it was the responsibility of the captain to keep costs to a minimum, which might lead to a temptation to cut corners in terms of safety measures. The British Board of Trade had strict standards and procedures for the safe operation of vessels and, if a ship was lost, a rigorous formal inquiry would be held to ascertain the cause and, if necessary, allocate blame. The owners of the ships could be fined and qualified crew could lose their certificates of competency.

Catherine's family liked Robert, but were disturbed by the idea of her marrying a sailor who would be away from home for months or years at a time. She was nearly 20 and her family thought she was a starry-eyed romantic. They hoped that, in time, she would forget him and his, in their view hasty, proposal of marriage. But she never did, and those two years of waiting seemed like an eternity to her, as she counted off the days to his unpredictable return. Catherine was not to know, but whilst she was waiting impatiently for Robert, the *Criccieth Castle* was experiencing some narrow escapes from disaster.

After leaving Newcastle in New South Wales she was almost capsized by a cyclone that hit when she was near to Norfolk Island in the Pacific, 2,000 miles east of Australia. In that incident she lost many sails and most of her lifeboats, but was able to limp on to Valparaiso, her next port of call. Here in August

1906 the ship was anchored off Valparaiso when an earthquake hit the town, destroying buildings and ships in the harbour. Somewhat battered but intact she eventually returned safely, arriving in Barry, South Wales, on 8th March 1907 having first delivered her cargo to Dunkirk.

The crew of the Criccieth Castle (year unknown)

Chapter 2

CATHERINE'S FIRST VOYAGE (1907 – 1908)

One morning in March 1907 Catherine was thrilled to receive a telegram from Robert to say that he had arrived in Barry and hoped that she would meet him there so they could get married before he had to sail again. Catherine wasted no time in taking what would be the biggest step of her life. Within a few short days she left her job, hurriedly packed a suitcase, said goodbye to her family and took the complicated train journey south, to Robert and the unknown. When she arrived they were both relieved to find that they still felt the same about each other. They were married in a quiet ceremony on March 26th 1907 at Cardiff Registry Office – neither of their families was able to make the long journey. Robert was 28 and Catherine was 22.

In the days before the wedding, Catherine had surprised Robert by announcing that she would not be returning to North Wales when he went to sea again, but that she would be coming with him. She knew from conversations with sailors' wives in Criccieth and Porthmadog that sometimes, though not very often, a captain's wife was able to join her husband on his voyages and she had been delighted when she learned that Richard Davies, the captain with whom Robert had served as first mate, was taking over as captain of another of Messrs Thomas' ships, the *Milverton*, and Robert was to be the new captain of the *Criccieth Castle*, making it possible for her to join him on board.

Robert took some persuading as his feelings were mixed. He was delighted at the prospect of having a companion to share the long days and nights of the voyages that went on for months on end, but he was also worried about how Catherine would take to a life at sea – it was far beyond her experience, there would be no turning back and how could either of them know what the future would bring.

Now loaded with a cargo of coal, the ship waited in the

At daylight they made sail and cast off the tug (R D Cadwalader)

harbour to take them on their honeymoon voyage to South America. When she first stood on the ship's deck with Robert, Catherine was so excited and overcome with happiness that she could hardly speak. But Robert understood. He was looking forward to feeling the motion of the deck rolling gently to the rhythm of the waves, the sound of the filling sails above and the tang of the salt wind in his face. These were feelings that Robert had known and loved all his life.

There were 27 people on the ship including six apprentices, three mates, a steward, cook, sailmaker, carpenter, and twelve ABs (Able-Bodied seamen). Robert was now signed on as the 'master' or captain of the *Criccieth Castle* and Catherine signed on as 'stewardess' earning just one shilling a month. The crew liked and respected their captain and, as the only woman on board, Catherine became mother, nurse and confidante to them.

They left Barry Dock on a nasty, drizzly Friday morning at 0500, and anchored in the 'Roads'. The Barry Roads were just clear of the lock gates and ships going to sea would change their dock pilots here for sea pilots. The crew spent the whole day tensioning the lanyards attached to the new main rigging that had been fitted in Barry. This tensioning was not only for the new set up – it was also necessary to adjust the rigging as the ship and cargo would settle and move about once she left port. The crew were getting quite adept at this as they had been working with the riggers for a few days before they left Barry. The men packed up at 1730 and were told to get their supper, while the mate organised the anchor watches for the night. They had just entered the forecastle with their supper, when someone said there was a tug, the *Persia* belonging to Watkins of London, making its way towards them. Sure enough there she was, coming to tow the *Criccieth Castle* down the Channel past Lundy Island. The voyage was about to begin.

There was no time for supper as the anchor had to be raised. 'Heave up; man the capstan,' was the order. Robert and his officers knew that the hard work would become easier if the men were occupying their minds by singing a sea shanty. 'Come on, boys! Make a noise. Raise her with a song.' But it was no use. Having left their loved ones and the many pleasures of being onshore, no one could put any heart into it. The poor mate, responsible for the raising of the anchor, was frantic. Even Mr Griffiths, the third mate, a tip-top shantyman, could not get any response from the crew. Captain Thomas could stand this no longer and sent the steward forward with a good tot of liquor for each man, and *then* the music started. With 'Fire Down Below', 'South Australia', 'Rolling River' and other tunes, they raised the anchor happy and smiling. Catherine had never seen anything like this and she was thrilled to hear the men singing as they worked the capstan. At last they were under way and were towed westwards through the night. At daylight they made sail and cast off the tug but kept the pilot aboard until they were clear of the Bristol Channel.

For the first few days Catherine was seasick, which made her very miserable and helpless, especially as she knew she would not see dry land again for months. Robert tried to persuade her to go back to Cardiff in the pilot's boat but she would not hear of it. Fortunately they had a nice cabin with oak bulkheads, a fitted red carpet, sideboard, table and chairs, and a double bunk where Catherine could lie, feeling awful with her seasickness. When she recovered, their routine was to rise at six for a cold bath, after which Robert would go to check the ship and its progress. They would take breakfast when he returned below at eight.

Catherine had been at sea for over a week when she experienced her first storm. It was frightening with the waves crashing down in the darkness and the vessel lurching violently from side to side. She stayed in the cabin, as every time she tried to reach Robert, up on deck, the unaccustomed movements threw her down. This was probably for the best as the *Criccieth Castle* was known for being a 'wet' ship, with water sluicing the decks with each big wave. Eventually, the storm blew itself out.

From the Bristol Channel they were now heading for Chile using the northeast Portuguese trade winds which would take them across the Atlantic Ocean towards the South American

She was known for being a 'wet' ship (R D Cadwalader)

coast. They passed St Paul's Rocks, a small archipelago in mid-Atlantic, about 500 miles off the coast of Brazil and just north of the equator at approximate longitude 30° W. This point of reference allowed them to confirm the accuracy of their chronometers which were crucial to the navigation of the voyage.

South of St Paul's Rocks was the area known as the doldrums, a large area of sea where the winds would drop or even disappear. Some ships became trapped here for several weeks as the weather systems passed round, but not through, the doldrums.

Eventually they neared the southern tip of South America, notorious for savage storms caused by the meeting of cold air from the Antarctic with the moist winds of the south Atlantic. They needed to pass through these seas and round Cape Horn, in Tierra del Fuego, to reach their destination in Chile, on the western side of South America.

However, before they could face this challenge, a member of crew spotted a wisp of smoke coming from a ventilator to the holds. Investigation showed that the cargo of coal was seriously overheating and, in places, was on fire. This was always a serious risk with such cargos, as Robert knew only too well from his dreadful experience on the *Eivion*. The problem was extensive, so he decided to turn back to Stanley on the Falkland Islands in order to quench the fire and unload and reload the holds, an impossible task out on the wild south Atlantic. Unfortunately the weather, already bad, was getting worse by the hour and the adverse winds, accompanied by snow squalls and poor visibility, forced them northwards and they ran for Montevideo in Uruguay instead.

To compound Robert's problems the ship was behaving strangely on her new course, being sluggish on the helm and slow to raise her bows from the cascading waves. The bosun was sent forward to investigate and was horrified to find the forepeak compartment was sloshing with tons of water.

Fearing that this weight would drag the ship under, the captain called on 'All Hands' to begin bailing. Each watch team had an empty meat cask slung on ropes which they lowered through the forepeak hatch and hauled up when full of water, to empty on to the deck where it sluiced away. This time there was no problem in getting the crew to sing and the strains of 'One More River to Cross' rang out as they strained on the ropes and pulleys. They kept this up for several hours and managed to get the water level much lower, but clearly there was a serious leak. The ship's sailmaker made two draw buckets out of canvas, smaller than the barrels and easier to manoeuvre in the restricted space. The work carried on with these for several more hours, but they had reached a point where the water level did not fall as the water was coming in as fast as they could bail. Something had to be done to raise her head so that she could make way; also the weather was getting worse. The captain then gave orders to open up the forehatch and dump some of the cargo overboard.

The bosun called for volunteers to go into the fume-filled holds and load buckets and barrels with the hot coal to be hauled up and thrown overboard. It was so bad that men could only stay below for a few minutes before emerging, choking, into the wild Atlantic weather. However, there was no shortage of volunteers as everybody recognised the seriousness of their situation. As the level of coal was reduced, the heat and fumes increased and eventually nobody could work below. Fortunately by then the ship was in better trim and responding to the helm so the captain gave the order to batten down the hatches and block all the ventilators to the holds. In this state they carried on and made it safely to Montevideo where they found themselves in the company of a few other 'lame ducks'.

When they were in the harbour the cause of the leak in the forepeak was discovered by the carpenter. A barrel of oil had broken adrift and been thrown around the forepeak by the violent movement of the ship. It had smashed one of the ship's pumps, allowing water to enter through the outlet pipe. It was an example of how attention to detail, or lack of it, could have very serious consequences in the extreme conditions faced by these ships.

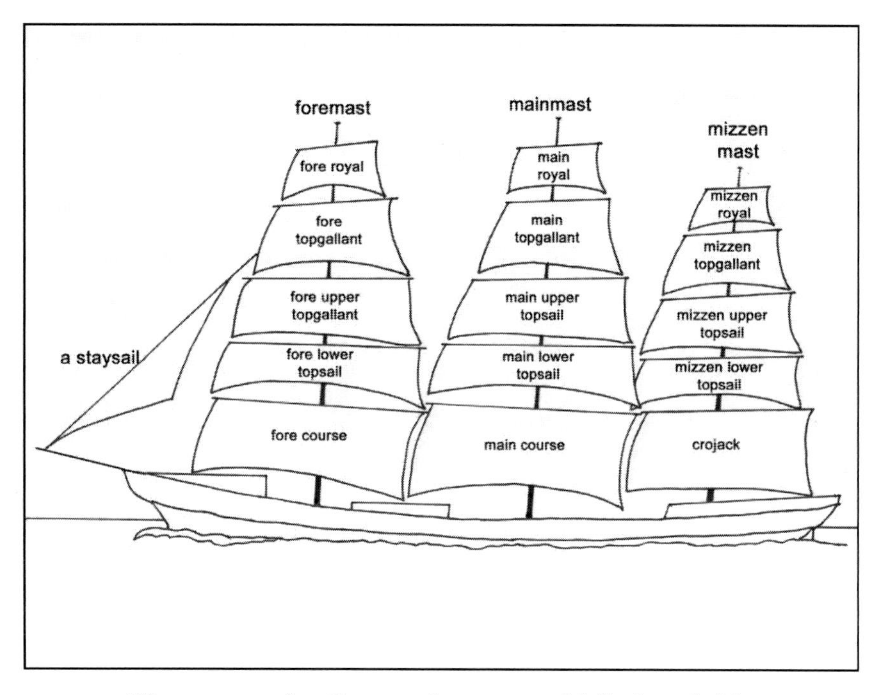

The masts and sails on a three-masted full-rigged ship

Having 'turned' the cargo to cool it down and undertaken the necessary repairs to the pump they left once more for Chile. Sadly they had to leave the 56-year-old second mate, Owen Jones from Pwllheli, at Montevideo. During a storm one of the spare spars kept on deck had come loose and both of Jones' legs were smashed when a wave washed him under the spar as he struggled to fix it. They heard later that he had died from gangrene shortly after the ship left. The third mate was promoted to second mate, and a new Spanish third mate was taken on at Montevideo.

Once they reached the 'Corner' (Cape Horn) they had the usual hard time of it. It was especially difficult sailing from east to west around the Horn as they were going against the prevailing winds and currents. To avoid the worst of the conditions they went very far south, well below 60° latitude. In the Antarctic winter the braces and running gear became coated in ice making them up to twice their normal thickness and causing them to jam in the blocks. Once, whilst 'heaving her to', the weather doors of the deck house were shattered and the forecastle and galley were washed out by the waves breaking over the decks. One of the boats on the deck house was smashed to matchwood. Every stitch of the crews' clothing was sodden and there was no place to dry anything. The off-duty watch made use of the sail locker to sleep, turning in wet and turning out steaming!

On a Sunday evening, after getting far enough to westward of the Horn, they had a favourable wind from the south and were bowling along with all sails set. At about 1930 the mate, seeing a squall on the horizon and realising the need to reduce the sail area, shouted, 'Clew up fore and mizzen royals. Haul the crojack up. Then all hands shorten sail.' The wind quickly freshened and with it came sleet and the men found, whilst going aloft to make the sails fast, that the rigging was thick with ice. There were layers and layers of sleet freezing as it touched and they all knew that the weight of ice aloft could destabilise and even capsize the ship. They shortened down to three lower topsails and were just about to go for a smoke, when away went the main lower topsail sheet. Before they could get the sail clewed up, the broken links of the chain sheet had slashed the brand new sail, and they only managed to save the roping. It sounded like a lot of machine guns going off and the threads of the canvas froze solid all over the rigging. Most of the running gear had been chopped off clean, getting washed overboard through the washports.

At last that was forgotten when they first saw their decks dry as they sailed north again to better weather; the decks had been awash with water for weeks. Eventually they arrived at Tocopilla where they commenced discharging their cargo of coal. After they had got 'skin' (reached the wood that lined the hold) and the coal clear from around the mainmast, they found the heel of the mast had been strained. One of the plates running across thwartships from the keelson under the first step of the mast was badly buckled. The Lloyd's representative and various ships' captains surveyed it; amongst them was the captain of the *Scottish Moors*. He was the proud 'Cracker Jack' or Top-Dog of the coast, as he was renowned for having recently beaten the *Potosi* in an informal race from Hamburg to Coquimbo, 400 miles south of Tocopilla. Another captain was from the *Kate Thomas*, a large four-masted barque owned by William Thomas of Anglesey and Liverpool. Two and a half years later in April 1910 the *Kate Thomas* sank off Land's End after a collision with another ship. The captain from Caernarfon and the mate from Pwllheli both had their wives on board when the steamer *India* collided with the *Kate Thomas* and everyone on the sailing ship was drowned apart from one apprentice. See Appendix XIV for an account of the tragedy.

The conclusion of the group of expert visitors was that the problem was not serious and the mast was passed fit for service. The crew finished discharging the coal and were looking forward to the fun that often took place when the last bit of the cargo was taken ashore. They were about to cheer the last basket of coal as it went out of the ship but as the basket was hoisted over the rail the youngest member of the crew, Geoffrey Dickson, a 16-year-old apprentice from Sunderland, jumped onto it with the Union Jack in his hand. He was then raised up high enough for the other ships in the harbour to see him and he shouted at the top of his voice, 'Three cheers for the captain, officers and crew of the *Criccieth Castle*'. He was then lowered and hoisted three times, while wildly waving his flag, and, before he and the basket were lowered onto the quay, he called for 'Three cheers for all the ships in the harbour'. A similar ceremony would take place with the last bit of cargo loaded on board.

Several days before the *Criccieth Castle* was due to leave, the *Scottish Moors* completed her loading and the ceremony to mark the leaving of a ship that was homeward bound began. At 2000 the 'homeward bounder', on this occasion the *Scottish Moors*, started to ring her bell. Immediately all the ships responded by ringing their poop and forecastle bells as loudly as possible for ten minutes. During this time the homeward bounder proceeded to raise on her foremast a wooden framework with lit riding lights in the form of the constellation of the 'Southern Cross'. This marked the start of the cheering. The crew member with the mightiest voice on the homeward bounder sang out, 'Three cheers for the *Kate Thomas*' (the name of the nearest vessel), with the cheers followed by the *Kate Thomas* replying, 'Three cheers for the homeward bounder!' The ceremony went on until every ship in the harbour had been cheered and given her cheers for the *Scottish Moors*. Then the *Scottish Moors* let off some fireworks and sent a boat around all the nearest ships with a bottle of grog for each.

Robert and Catherine joined all the other captains, several of whom also had their wives with them, on the *Scottish Moors* to be entertained by her captain. Many apprentices were on the deck having rowed their captains across the harbour. Before leaving, the 'Southern Cross' was lowered down and everyone on board joined in to sing the 'Homeward Bound' shanty:

O fare you well, I wish you well!

Good-bye, fare you well; good-bye, fare you well!

O, fare you well, my bonny young girls!

Hoorah, my boys, we're homeward bound!

Soon the *Criccieth Castle* would also be ready to leave Chile. The bags of saltpetre (nitrates) had been carefully counted at each hold by a shoreside tallyman with one of the mates and an apprentice posted beside each tallyman to check his counting. The mate sometimes checked the weight of a sample of the bags; onshore or onboard. Eventually everyone was satisfied and the Bills of Lading were signed so that the captain and consigner would have copies, and a copy could be sent to the consignee. These certificates stated the number of bags the *Criccieth Castle* was charged with carrying to 'Falmouth for orders'. Many ships returning to Europe with cargos after months or even years away would first call at Falmouth in Cornwall. This was because

Falmouth is an excellent deep water harbour, it had good provisioning, there were skilled ship repairers and it also had a fine fleet of tug-boats. At Falmouth the consignees of the cargo would be contacted by telegram and they would let the ship captains know which port to take their cargo to. Once at this port the consignee's bill of lading would be compared with the captain's before the ships were unloaded.

At last it was the *Criccieth Castle*'s turn to hoist the 'Southern Cross' and to cheer all the ships in the harbour. The next morning they set off for home. They had to head out westwards into the Pacific for several hundred miles to avoid the strong north-flowing Peru Current, also known as the Humboldt Current, before turning south. Several weeks later at 0500 on Christmas Day they sighted the Horn and later that morning they overtook a four-masted steel barque, the *Holt Hill*, passing her to starboard. In the afternoon they started to shorten down their topsails, and had the pleasure of seeing the Horn and the *Holt Hill* with everything set way to the west of them. The *Criccieth Castle* had the advantage because she could take a course closer to the wind.

Weeks later off the river Plate between Argentina and Uruguay they had a big blow or *pampero* as the polar wind here is sometimes called, and they lost some more sails. After the blow died away the seas rose and they did a fair amount of rolling!

With no wind, the uncontrolled movements of the ship caused some severe damage. At 0400 there was a crash in the vicinity of the mainmast. The bosun shouted, 'All hands!' so the crew knew it was something serious. They tumbled out, and on going aft, saw the top of the main mast swinging upside down like a pendulum about three feet clear of the main hatch; the top horizontal spar, the royal yard, was in two halves, with one yardarm stuck into the hatch and the topgallant yard through their lower topsail. What a mess! The fore royal and mizzen royal yards were sprung, besides the fore and mizzen topgallant braces being carried away. Whilst they were clearing the wreckage a ship passed and asked if they required any assistance, which was declined with thanks, and after a busy day they limped on again as a 'lame duck'. Somewhere near the equator, or the 'Line' as they called it, while they were becalmed in the doldrums, a steamer, the *SS Alston,* closed with them and using a speaking trumpet asked where and how they had lost their main topmast, and whether they required any food or water. Again this kind offer was declined with thanks. The *Alston* pressed on, Mr Wyatt, her captain, promising to report their position and cirmumstances at St Vincent.

St Vincent is one of the Cape Verde Islands and was very important for communication at the beginning of the twentieth century as it had a telegraph station which connected it to other stations by underwater cables. These cables were laid on the seabed between telegraph stations stretching right around the globe. The cables were used to transmit messages in Morse Code using electrical impulses. These were standardized sequences of short and long signals called 'dots' and 'dashes' which could be converted back into words at the receiving stations and they made communications extremely fast. The *Alston* would have communicated with the telegraph station using flags, flashing lights or a message may have been physically taken to the island. A telegram concerning the whereabouts and condition of the *Criccieth Castle* would then have been sent from St Vincent to Fayal on the Azores along the seabed cables and from there to Porthcurno near Land's End in Cornwall. From here the message would go overland to the company's office in Liverpool.

The steamer was not out of sight before the *Criccieth Castle* felt a breeze which they hoped would herald that they had entered the northeast trades, the winds that if they remained steady on the beam would take them in the direction they wanted to go. From then until they reached Falmouth they were hardly without a leading wind and to have such a continuously favourable air current was deemed amazingly lucky.

The Criccieth Castle was towed up the river to Antwerp
(R D Cadwalader)

On the morning they arrived off Falmouth, the tug *Triton* came alongside and they asked her the name of the full-rigged ship they saw outside of them. They were told it was one of the Liverpool 'Scottishes'. After towing the *Criccieth Castle* in and getting her moored, the tug went out to the other ship. There was huge surprise on board when they saw the tug towing in the *Scottish Moors* last seen leaving Tocopilla several days before they left. There was plenty of cheering and bell ringing. Another ship in the same tier could not make out what all the noise was about, but joined in with the 'music' just the same. Good old *Criccieth Castle*! The 'old crock' had beaten the 'Cracker Jack' home. Their rival had had a head-start but the *Criccieth Castle* had made the passage in a fast 101 days despite having been crippled.

They stopped in Falmouth for three days. The message then arrived from the consignee giving them 'orders for Antwerp', that is, they were to take their cargo of nitrates to Antwerp. They were towed there, as was normal practice in the Channel, and apart from being nearly run down on the way, their troubles and excitement from this voyage were over. Passing Dungeness they spotted the *SS Alston.* Captain Wyatt could not believe his eyes when he saw them and altered course to congratulate them on their smart passage from the 'Line'. The steamer had discharged her cargo at Rotterdam and was bound for Barry in ballast.

On a Sunday afternoon the *Criccieth Castle* was towed up the river to Antwerp in company with the *Pegasus, Holt Hill* and *Arracan*, all four-masted ships. The crew members from all the ships were paid off and they returned to Britain on the Harwich ferry, the *SS Colchester*, on the Monday night. What singing resulted from the four combined windjammer crews, something for the other passengers to remember, some of whom kept the sailors 'well primed' to keep the music flowing.

Edmund Howard, the AB, who wrote about this voyage 25 years later and a long time after the *Criccieth Castle* had been lost, said of Catherine, 'I consider her one of the pluckiest women I know. To think what she went through that voyage and to go back again until the ship finally foundered proved her to be a stout-hearted, plucky woman. I raise my hat to her and hope she enjoys good health and prosperity.'

Chapter 3

BOBBY'S FIRST VOYAGE (1909 – 1911)

At the end of this first long voyage together Robert and Catherine bought a house in Llangybi called Gorsannedd, just down the lane from the post office where Catherine grew up. In less than a month Robert had to set off on his next voyage and Catherine, who was now six months pregnant, stayed at home to have the baby.

Robert travelled back to Antwerp to commence his next voyage on the re-rigged *Criccieth Castle* on April 11th 1908. There were eight apprentices on this voyage, the first one for two 16-year-olds – Frederick Sainsbury Lord from Leith and Fred Upham Hellyer from Hull. From Antwerp they sailed to Barry in South Wales to load up with coal. The crew agreement contained a special clause that 'all ABs and men rated as sailors and signing on at Barry, who make the round voyage in the ship shall be paid a bonus of five shillings each per month from the date of joining'. On this voyage only one man deserted and this was after they had sailed without mishap all the way to Chile, to a town called Mejillones where they arrived on October 24th to discharge their cargo and load up with nitrates to Falmouth for orders. The voyage ended on April 13th 1909 at Antwerp.

Meanwhile on 18th June 1908 Catherine gave birth to their first baby – a boy, who they had decided to call Robert or Bobby for short. Robert was gone for twelve months and Bobby was nearly ten months old before his father saw him for the first time. He took one look at the little boy and said, 'He's going to be a sailor!'

One morning a few weeks later the details of Robert's next voyage arrived in the post. 'You'll have to stay at home with Bobby,' he told Catherine. Then, as he saw her disappointment, he went on, 'You can't take a baby to sea. Anything might happen.' Catherine, however, was again determined that the sea would not separate her from her husband. She would set up home and bring up a family on his ship – in spite of all the dangers that she knew existed. Ships in those days were completely cut off from the world for months on end. There was no radar, no electricity or gas, no means of communication and none of the comforts that are taken for granted today. Also the casualty rate at sea was incredibly high. People died from diseases or accidents. Ships caught fire and many just disappeared.

Even knowing the risks and having experienced her first eventful voyage, Catherine knew that whatever happened she would not be happy unless she was by her husband's side and, despite everything that occurred later, she never regretted her decision to stay with him.

So, having been persuaded to let them join him, Robert returned to Antwerp in May, and Catherine and Bobby joined the *Criccieth Castle* in Cardiff when she arrived there at the end of June 1909, just after Bobby's first birthday.

They were bound for Chile again and their first port of call after rounding Cape Horn was the port of Taltal. They arrived there on 1st November 1909 to collect a cargo of Chilean nitrates. Two of the crew had to leave the ship here on medical grounds. One of them was the 33-year-old second mate Arthur Hoar from Falmouth who was suffering from venereal disease. Before the ship left, his pay of £6.18s.3d, his effects and Discharge Certificate were delivered to him on shore. The ship then set sail to cross the Pacific Ocean bound for Australia, arriving at Newcastle in New South Wales on 24th February 1910. For reasons not specified in the ship's papers two men were taken off the ship and put in gaol and their wages and effects were left at the Shipping Office. Six other crew members deserted and three left by mutual consent. One of these was the first mate Richard Jones from Caernarfon and he was replaced by H Godwin, a 42-year-old New Zealander.

They now recrossed the Pacific with a cargo of coal to arrive again in Chile, this time at Valparaiso, on 28th June 1910. It was just after Bobby's second birthday and the little boy had spent a whole year, half his life, at sea. Along the coast from Valparaiso at Caleta Coloso they again loaded a cargo of Chilean saltpetre to take to Italy. It took them four months to round the Horn and arrive at Gibraltar on their way to Leghorn on the northwest coast of Italy very close to Pisa. (Note that Livorno was traditionally known as Leghorn, a corruption of its ancient Italian name Legorno, to foreign sailors.) Godwin the first mate was suffering from pneumonia and had to be left in the hospital at Gibraltar. He was replaced by William A Gale, a 26-year-old from Ramsey on the Isle of Man. Gale was an experienced seaman although his father, John, was an agricultural labourer.

Bobby was a born sailor. He did not get seasick, he hardly ever cried, and it had not been long before he had started toddling around on deck with the sailors, who made a big fuss of him. He enjoyed feeding scraps to the various livestock that were kept on board to provide occasional fresh food, often chickens and sometimes a pig or two. In less than two years Bobby had been to South America, Australia, back to South America and finally to the Mediterranean. The ports of call there were as romantic as they sounded with brightly coloured houses with old women in black shawls sitting in the doorways. Many of the houses around the ports were decorated using whatever paint the occupants could get from the visiting ships.

Those years and the years that followed were the happiest of Catherine's life. She was in love, she had a handsome little son, and, as they set off on their third trip to South America she could not believe that anything could possibly destroy their happiness.

William Gale, the mate (WWM 1913)

Chapter 4

OUTWARD VOYAGE (1911 – 1912)

They left Leghorn in March 1911. At Leghorn the *Criccieth Castle* had been drydocked, cleaned, painted and the rudder rebushed. William Gale was again taken on as the first mate, normally referred to as the 'mate', and his pay was £8 a month, the highest of all the 20 crew. There were four apprentices including Lord and Hellyer who were now 19 years old. The rest of the crew as usual came from a mix of backgrounds, a typical example being the cook and steward, Peter Subra. Subra grew up in Bethnal Green in London where his French father was a feather dresser preparing feathers ready to sell. Subra was the youngest of six children and after leaving school he trained to become a cook while living at home and then later became a 'marine cook'.

As on her other voyages Catherine was listed as a member of the crew on the crew agreement. She was still a 'stewardess' with a payment of only one shilling per month.

From Leghorn they sailed to Porto Empedocle in Sicily, where they took on a cargo of sulphur to carry to Port Pirie in South Australia. There the sulphur would be used to make fertilizers, explosives and for use in the mining industry. In 1911 Broken Hill Association Smelters was the largest lead smelting company in the world. It had engaged some of the best industrial chemists available to develop the cutting edge technology used in the extraction process of lead and other metals from the galena ore that was mined there.

They sailed through the Mediterranean, stopping at Gibraltar to discharge Evan Jones, the 64-year-old second mate from Porthmadog. J Parry from Birkenhead was taken on as carpenter. Since they now had no second mate it is likely that Frederick, the senior apprentice, acted in this 'rank', probably backed up by the bosun, until his apprenticeship was completed on 8th April in the following year, 1912.

Robert, Bobby and Catherine in Port Pirie, November 1911 (WWM 1913)

While at Gibraltar Catherine had time to look around the small town. She loved the narrow streets, the quaint shops and the busy excitement. When Robert told her that they had been invited to dinner with the Governor, she had to rummage through her cases to find the beautiful embroidered tulle dress she kept for her rare social occasions. They set off for the large white stone mansion, known as 'The Convent', where they sat out on the veranda and had a magnificent meal. All too soon for Catherine they were leaving Gibraltar.

They set the sails of the *Criccieth Castle* to take them well out into the Atlantic, passing north of Madeira. From here they would pick up the northeast Portuguese trade winds which would take them southwest to the South American coast, passing St Paul's Rocks. They slogged across the doldrums and picked up the prevailing southwest trade winds down to latitude 40° S, well south of the Cape of Good Hope, and then ran eastwards half way round the world along the 'Roaring Forties' to Australia. They at last arrived in South Australia in September after a decent time of 103 days from Gibraltar. The ship lay at anchor in one of the many anchorages in Spencer Gulf before finally entering Port Pirie harbour on 9th October 1911.

After the crew had discharged the cargo of sulphur they swept and washed out the hold until it was spotless, as wheat was to be the next cargo. This was a horrible job and may have tipped the balance for some of the crew who were already considering jumping ship in Australia.

Before loading the wheat, the shipper sent a surveyor to inspect the hold and bilges.

Port Pirie was a busy port situated on the dry hot flat coast 140 miles north of Adelaide. Its main street had some impressive buildings. While here Captain Thomas, Catherine and Bobby had their photograph taken by a local photographer at Duryea's Studio. A photograph was also taken of three-year-old Bobby sitting on a pretend crow's nest.

Only one man was officially discharged in Port Pirie. He was Arthur Andrews, an AB from Manchester, and he was paid a total of £21.4s.8d for his services. However, 14 other crew members made the decision to desert at this port and they left the ship without any pay. Of these men, records in Port Pirie show that two Russian Finns, who deserted on the day the ship cleared harbour, 14th November 1911, were sentenced by the local Police Court to 14 days' imprisonment for desertion. The men may have deserted because they only wanted a 'free' passage to Australia, perhaps they disliked the ship or maybe the daunting prospect of rounding the Horn in winter on the return voyage would have been a factor. Whatever the reasons they all left without getting paid. Desertions were by no means untypical. In the 1850s whole crews, including the officers, jumped ship to go to the Victorian gold fields, and again in the 1890s crew members left for the Kalgoorlie gold rush in Western Australia.

Ships in Port Pirie Harbour (courtesy of Tony Jones, Golau Llŷn Light)

Of the four apprentices two, Millar and Read, also deserted in Port Pirie. It was the mate's job to approve of replacements as he was in charge of the crew. He would try to get all ABs but as there was such a turnover generally with men deserting, dying of disease and accidents, he would often have no choice but to take on inexperienced men (often disparagingly called 'farmers' or 'soldiers') or men without discharge books or papers. These men would be rated as plain 'sailors'. Fourteen new crew were signed on at Port Pirie. They were five ABs, one carpenter, one boy, one cabin boy and six sailors, and all of these crew signed on with the Agreement that they would be discharged in Callao, or Calio as it was referred to then, their next destination in Peru, a few miles from the capital, Lima.

The *Criccieth Castle* was fixed (chartered) to load wheat to take across the Pacific Ocean to Callao. Grain was a dangerous cargo as it did not fill the hold before the vessel had reached its load-line, the legal limit to which a ship may be loaded for specific water types and temperatures. Wheat was very liable to shift and destabilise the ship, so to combat this the loose grain was covered with several layers of bagged wheat.

It was also important to make sure that wheat could not get into the sump around the bilge pumps because wheat, once wet, would expand and could prevent the pumps from working. The bilge covers had holes in them for drainage of water from the holds and these needed to be covered in burlap as a filter to stop the wheat falling through.

On November 14th 1911 they left Port Pirie and sailed down Spencer Gulf past Kangaroo Island, then south of Tasmania and New Zealand, and east along latitude 50° S in the southern part of the Pacific Ocean where they could catch the Westerlies, until they found the southeast trades that they could use to head northeast to arrive finally at Callao. They were also helped by the South Pacific Current and then the Peru or Humboldt Current. On reaching the Spanish-speaking port of Callao and discharging their cargo, all the men taken on at Port Pirie were paid off under their Terms of Agreement, receiving on average £15 for their three months' work.

So once again new crew were needed! Of the original crew of 26 taken on at Leghorn and Gibraltar nearly a year before,

Three-year-old Bobby on a pretend crow's nest (WWM 1913)

besides Robert and Catherine, only six remained: the first mate, William Gale, two Finnish ABs, Samuel Numiquiner (27 years) and Kusta Laine (26 years), the 53-year-old cook and steward, Peter Subra, and the two remaining apprentices who were soon to be promoted. Both were now 20 years old. On 8th April 1912 the first one, Frederick Sainsbury Lord, officially became second mate. This was exactly four years from the date of his indenture to the Ship Criccieth Castle Company on 8th April 1908. He would now receive wages – as an apprentice he would not have been paid – and his name was added to the crew agreement which he had to sign. Lord's family now lived in Sunderland where his father was a prevention officer for HM Customs, and he had several brothers and a sister. On 19th May the one remaining apprentice, Fred Upham Hellyer, was made third mate, and this too was exactly four years since he had started his indenture. Fred was from Hull where his father was a sailmaker and he had two older sisters.

Soon the mate was supervising the signing on of the new men. There was Osterstram, a 41-year-old Swedish carpenter, and Westerberg, a 45-year-old Finnish sailmaker, plus thirteen others. Nakarate from Japan, although 25 years of age, was taken on as cabin boy. There were seven British men including William Summers, an AB of 21 years from Dundee, and J Roberts, a married AB of 38 years from Holyhead on Anglesey. J W Wilson, 43 years and from Jersey, became the new bosun. Also joining were J Arnfors and H Kinnunen, both Finnish ABs of 21 and 24 years, Juan Cecchi, an Italian 19-year-old OS or Ordinary Seaman, who was too young to be an AB, and a 23 year Swede called C Borjerson. T Barker, at 56 the oldest member to join the crew and from Rhode Island in USA, and finally a 20-year-old German AB called Kannegiesser joined the ship.

From Callao the *Criccieth Castle* sailed 100 miles down the coast of Peru in ballast to the Islas Ballestas. These islands lie some ten miles off the coast. The area looks very barren but the meeting of the cold Humboldt Current with the warmer tropical currents off-coast means that plankton and nutrients are swept up from the ocean floor and provide rich feeding grounds for the sea life. As a consequence of this, phenomenal numbers of seabirds live on the bountiful pickings. Over the centuries the droppings from the seabirds collected in enormous quantities, and the very dry climate meant that they were not washed away. Incas and the following Spanish-speaking Peruvians used the droppings called 'guano' as a fertiliser. It was the explorer Humboldt who in 1802 took the news of the huge quantities and the rich nitrate content of the guano to the outside world. Thus began the guano trade, not only for its role as a rich soil fertiliser, but also for its use in producing gunpowder.

A wooden structure on one of the Ballestas Islands used for loading ships with guano

At Ballestas they had to take on board 2,850 tons of guano in bulk for which they already had orders to take to Antwerp.

While the ship was being loaded, the captain with Catherine and Bobby went to Pisco, a town on the mainland of Peru about 12 miles due east of the Ballestas Islands. This was a welcome relief from the arid islands with their thousands of seabirds. Robert had to go to Pisco to get an 'outward clearance' document from the customs indicating all duties had been paid. The 'P' flag (Blue Peter) could then be flown which indicated that the vessel was clear to leave and showed any local shopkeepers that if they had an unsettled bill they had better get it sorted! Not very relevant on the bleak unpopulated Ballestas!

On completion of the loading the consignor appointed a load-line surveyor to witness the drafts and check the calculation of the tonnage loaded from the vessel's displacement tables. The ship now drew 21 feet 3 inches fore and aft with a freeboard of 4 feet $11^1/_2$ inches. The legal load-line or Plimsoll line was still $1^1/_2$ inches above water level, so the ship was by no means overloaded. The captain and mate would have calculated the displacement prior to the loading. The copies of the Bill of Lading were signed by the captain confirming the quantity of guano being shipped.

Chapter 5

TO CAPE HORN

Before leaving for Pisco, Robert had told the mate to ensure that the holds were properly cleaned out before the new cargo was loaded, and that the bilges were clear of anything that might block the pumps. Possibly the worst job on a ship was cleaning the bilges, made revolting by rotting bits of cargo and the occasional decomposing rat. The task was usually carried out by apprentices, under the supervision of the mate – all part of their learning the trade. However, at this time the Criccieth Castle had no apprentices as the two remaining ones had completed their training and had been promoted to second and third mates, so the mate had used a couple of reluctant ordinary seamen for the job. It was normal practice for the ship's carpenter to test the pumps before sailing.

A week after the ship sailed from Ballestas, the daily inspection found wheat in the bilges near the pump well – a serious problem as the swollen wheat could easily block the intake to the pumps. It was apparent that Robert's orders to clean up had not been properly carried out and, furthermore, Robert realised that the wheat could only have got into the bilges if the drain holes to the bilges had not been properly covered with burlap to filter any loose wheat from the drainage. This should have happened before the last cargo was loaded and the failures were evidence of careless work that could risk the lives of all aboard.

Realising the potential enormity of this neglect, the captain ordered this work to be undertaken at once in so far as it was then possible. The hatch covers were all sealed over the holds and these should not be removed once the ship was under way in case a heavy sea entered the hold. The only safe access to the hold was via the ventilators, curved funnel-shaped tubes. William Summers, the young AB from Dundee, was given the job of going into the hold to clear the bilges. He went down a ventilator, onto the fresh water tank immediately to the stern of the pump well, and from there descended to the bilge and began trying to clear out the wheat. He used a tin to bail a mixture of wheat and water which he put into a bucket to be hauled up through the ventilator from above. Coming up at intervals to the top of the water tank to rest and get purer air, he continued down there in the very confined space until his eyes and nose were bleeding from the effects of the foul wet guano stench and fumes of rotting wheat. Eventually after two hours he was forced to give up the attempt.

The pumps were retested but again very little water came out and what did come through was black and mixed with grain. The sounding rod showed there was still six inches of rotten wheat and water. A windsail was used to try to clear the fumes for another attempt at bailing. The second mate went down but owing to the gases and stench he came straight up again, confirming that conditions were nigh on impossible; and so reluctantly no further action was taken. Before too long the significance of all this was to return to haunt them.

Nothing untoward happened until they were abreast of Valparaiso when they encountered a very heavy southwest gale which lasted for 48 hours. They lost several new sails that were torn to ribbons by the force of the wind and the gig was dashed to pieces by waves crashing onto the deck. Hardly had the storm abated before the weather again turned black and another gale beat down upon them. This weather continued for a period of three weeks and they had a succession of fearful storms with gale force winds with hardly a break between them. The waves were mountainous and at times the captain ordered oil to be poured overboard to reduce the turbulence and the amount of water crashing on to the deck. Despite these storms, they safely weathered the Horn and everyone breathed more freely. They were looking forward to better weather as the strain upon them had been very severe.

The sky, however, was still overcast and the seas were

running high. On Sunday July 14th at about 2300 another storm sprang up from the northwest. The upper topsails were at once got in, and at midnight all hands furled the foresail and the ship was hove-to under lower topsails and storm staysails. The gale steadily increased in violence and huge seas were running. Catherine was lying awake with four-year-old Bobby in her arms, seasick and being thrown from side to side in the bunk. The ship was creaking and groaning as the waves lashed against the sides. It sounded as though the vessel was being ripped apart and all around, the wild green grey waves were cascading up and crashing down. She wondered how long the ship could survive.

At about two o'clock on the Monday morning there was a tremendous crash and the ship lurched forward. Catherine heard Robert's voice above the deafening roar of the storm – 'All hands on deck.'

The noise was terrifying and the captain was fearful that they had struck an iceberg or a part submerged wreck. He sent men forward to check, but they reported that all was clear at the bow. However, the helmsman shouted that the ship was not responding to the wheel – clearly something was seriously amiss with the steering gear; it was either broken or perhaps even carried away. He gave orders for rope tackles to be fixed on the tiller, to give more control, but these had no effect so he realised that it must be the connection to the rudder itself which had broken. A rapid inspection by the mate showed that the rudderstock was broken next to the iron horseshoe plate, presumably caused by a very heavy sea hitting the ship on the quarter. Any attempt at repair was impossible as it could only be done from a boat over the side, which was out of the question in such weather and seas.

The rudder was now out of control and striking heavily against the stops on port and starboard and its swinging was opening out the shell plates around the sternpost – a problem that could have been avoided if the ship was fitted with rudder chains to restrain this movement. These, however, were considered to be obsolete at this time and rarely fitted to ships of the *Criccieth Castle*'s generation. The constant heavy pounding and wrenching soon caused the shell plates to part from the sternpost entirely and water began to rush in through the opened seam. Robert sent the first mate to the after-hold to assess the situation below decks and he reported back that the ship was leaking all down the sternpost, with no possibility of stopping the flow from inside the vessel.

In the cabin, Bobby, shaking with fear, began crying softly to himself. Catherine, sensing the seriousness of the situation, did her best to comfort him. A few minutes later, Robert came below to say that the rudder was broken, which confirmed her fears of a serious problem.

With water pouring into the after-hold they needed to man the pumps but this proved impossible because the decks were being continually flooded by the heavy seas. In order to give the vessel more freeboard and raise the deck above the wave level they tried to jettison some cargo through the poop ventilators. It was unsafe to remove the hatch covers in such a high sea so the only access was through these ventilators. Volunteer crewmen awkwardly climbed below with buckets, which they filled with the guano ready to be thrown overboard.

After working incredibly hard for some hours, during which time they jettisoned several tons of cargo, they discovered to their dismay that the weight of water which had come in was in excess of the weight of cargo which had been thrown overboard, so that the ship had actually less freeboard than when they had started. This was most disheartening but not really surprising as it would take the shedding of 18 tons of cargo to lift the vessel an inch in the water. Their desperate efforts were in vain.

At four o'clock the weather began to improve, and by six o'clock the sea moderated sufficiently to allow the pumps to be manned. To their horror the crew found the pumps were almost useless because they had been choked with the wheat that had not been cleared prior to the loading. They persevered for an hour, but all in vain; the pumps refused to work and nothing could be done to prevent the ship from sinking.

She appeared like a huge living thing struggling for life (WWM 1913)

Chapter 6

ABANDONING SHIP

The Norwegian carpenter, Osterstram from Arendal, reported to the captain that there was four to five feet of water in the after-hold, and two-and-a-half feet in the hold amidships. It was clear to Robert that it was now impossible to keep the ship afloat much longer. The only choice to be made was to abandon ship and take to the boats as quickly as possible. The gig had already been smashed in, so they only had two boats left; the 26-foot lifeboat that could hold 34 persons and a 23-foot longboat that could hold 20 persons. The captain decided to split the ship's company between the two boats to give more room for each person and to have more freeboard in the rough seas. But how could they launch the boats without damaging them?

Although the weather had moderated since the time of the accident seven hours before, the sea was still running high and the vessel was rolling fearfully. The captain gave orders for the side of the ship to be padded in case the boats were banged against the hull by the heavy seas. Sails were taken from the sail-locker and lashed in place. Provisions and stores were gathered hastily and two kegs of water and enough biscuits for ten or twelve days, as well as a case of tinned meat, were placed in both boats.

Despite all their precautions they had a bad mishap while lowering the lifeboat. Catherine and Bobby along with the sailmaker, steward, and carpenter had been helped into it before it left the chocks. The ropes which were used as guys were new. Just as the davit tackles were being pulled upon, and while the boat was swinging, the ship gave a tremendous roll. Unfortunately this caused the new guys to stretch so much that the boat crashed against the davits with terrific force, straining the craft in every plank from keel to gunwale. The sudden and unexpected lurch nearly threw them all into the sea.

Fortunately the lifeboat was still seaworthy following this

incident, the damage could have been far worse and the boat could have been rendered useless. It was a very anxious time, but after further efforts they managed to get the boat into the water. Here it was repeatedly dashed against the padded side of the ship, and it was fortunate that the precaution of providing the soft bed had been taken, otherwise it would have been quickly pounded to pieces. The violent motion of the little craft on the high sea that was running caused Catherine to become very seasick, and she and Bobby sat helplessly in the bottom of the boat, saturated with ice-cold water. One minute the lifeboat would be level with the rail of the ship; and the next ten or fifteen feet below, tossed up and down on the great waves like a cork.

Robert shouted to Catherine and Bobby to be brave before he turned to supervise the launching of the longboat and getting the rest of the crew on board it. This was no easy task due to the rolling of the ship. Night was fast approaching and there was every appearance of the weather turning bad again. The wind and sea were gradually rising, the sky was overcast, and a cold drizzling rain was falling. The first mate, William Gale, was put in charge of the longboat with six of the crew. The longboat did not have a chart but they did have a compass. Before leaving the ship the captain showed the mate their position on the chart, which would be in the lifeboat, and told him the compass bearing for reaching the Falklands. The idea was to make for these islands which were about 180 miles away and the nearest reachable land. Although being well aware of the dangers of their situation in open leaky boats in one of the stormiest regions in the world in its bitterly cold mid-winter, the captain fully expected them all to pull through.

Before leaving his ship the captain did not want the ship's livestock to suffer through drowning and he shot the pig with his pistol, and wrung the necks of the remaining chickens. To ensure that the hulk of the ship did not become a hazard to shipping the afterhatch cover and poop skylights were opened so she would sink quickly.

The second mate (Lord), sailmaker (Westerburg), and ten seamen eventually joined Catherine and the others in the lifeboat, making 17 souls in all. When Robert stepped into the lifeboat the water was up to his knees, for the boat was leaking as a result of her planks being strained. At last they pushed off and pulled away.

Abandoning ship (R D Cadwalader)

When they last saw their gallant ship through the darkness she appeared like a huge living thing struggling for life, rolling heavily and pitching violently, with her decks aft nearly awash and the stern deep in the water. They got away only just in time.

Any delay and they would all have gone down with the vessel. And so the *Criccieth Castle* was left in the South Atlantic Ocean at about 1600 on Monday 15th July 1912 at approximately latitude 54° 14′ S and longitude 61° 24' W.

At 1700 the wind freshened to a gale. The longboat until then had been in the tow of the lifeboat with men in both boats pulling on their oars, but now it had to be cast off with instructions to keep in company if possible. The weather became worse and at about 1830 the longboat waved a light to show that there was a problem. The lifeboat thereupon got close to her, and the mate shouted that he had lost his tiller. The lifeboat had a spare one and this was thrown to him.

Unfortunately the gale was strengthening. By 2100 that night it was blowing a hurricane and the sea was running mountains high. The mate shouted that he was going to heave-to as his boat was taking in 'green' seas, not just spray. The captain replied that the lifeboat was also shipping water, but whilst he was securing a steering oar to its stern as they had now lost their rudder, the longboat disappeared from view. An attempt was made to show a light in the lifeboat but it constantly blew out. After 2130 they made no further attempts to light it. It was impossible to make any progress, and so the rowers in the lifeboat were ordered to heave-to and they set sea-anchors to which were attached bags full of oil. In the darkness they saw no light from the longboat, but fully expected to see her next morning, and it was Robert's intention to transfer two or three men to the longboat because the lifeboat was leaking so much.

In the first light of dawn after a miserable and anxious night, the mate's boat was nowhere to be seen. They scanned the horizon in every direction and speculated as to what had become of their companions, surmising all sorts of things. First of all they thought that they had been picked up by some passing ship, but finally came reluctantly to the conclusion that their frail craft had been capsized in the storm and all of them drowned. Possibly their boat had drifted some distance away before the catastrophe happened where any cries for help would have been inaudible amid the roar of the storm.

This tragedy saddened and dispirited those in the lifeboat beyond description. They were now left to fight for their lives alone, and a grim fight it was destined to be – against hunger and thirst, mountainous seas, and the freezing, numbing cold. Snow was now falling, accompanied by stinging showers of hail, and despite heavy clothing, oilskins and boots, they were all wet through to the skin. Indeed, it seemed to them miraculous that they had not all perished that first night, huddled up as they were with the icy water slopping around in the bottom of the labouring boat.

The sun rose and with it their spirits. And then something happened that gave them hope.

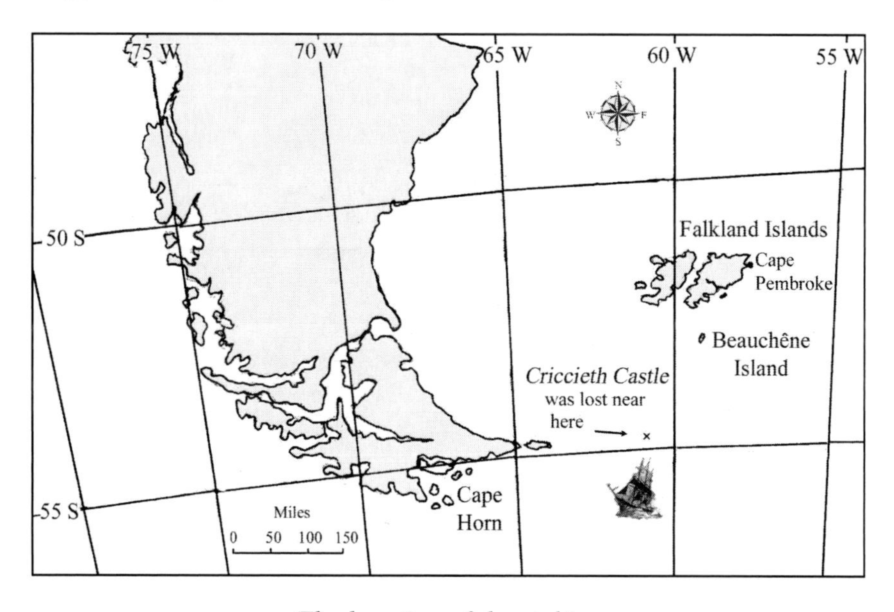

The location of the sinking

Chapter 7

A SHIP! A SHIP!

As they crested the waves they thought they caught glimpses of a sail. The sailors began to shout: 'A ship! A ship!' Soon they were able to identify the masts and sails of a four-masted barque which seemed to be sailing towards them.

The crew went wild shouting and waving (WWM 1913)

The crew went wild shouting and waving, and a blanket was hoisted as a distress signal. There were tears in the sailors' eyes as they thought their suffering would soon be over. To be rescued so quickly seemed too wonderful to be true. Catherine looked down at Bobby whose large frightened blue eyes watched her questioningly, but he did not say a word as she hugged him to her. Robert and Catherine smiled at each other, and his smile was the assurance that she needed. She had been desperately worried not only for Robert, Bobby and the crew, but also for her unborn child. She was now five months pregnant.

They watched every movement of the vessel which was so close they could see the sailors up in the rigging adjusting the sails and they shouted and called until they were hoarse. They could not believe that they would not be seen. 'Over here,' they shouted again and again, 'Help, help, for the love of God.' The men got so excited, seeing help so close, and worked themselves up into such a frenzied state the captain had to remonstrate with them, pointing out that if they acted so foolishly the disappointment, if they should not happen to be seen, would only tell upon them. His words were like a premonition and at last they realised they were not going to be rescued as the ship appeared to turn and eventually disappeared from sight. Had the barque seen them and decided to take no action to save them, or had they not been seen at all? Either answer led to the same outcome.

It seemed as if their last chance of survival had gone. They dared not think how they were to survive another night like the last one in the open lifeboat. What is more, the boat was now leaking so badly they had to throw all the canned meat overboard to lighten it.

Bitterly disappointed that they were not to be rescued and worn out with toil, hungry and paralysed with the cold, several of the men sank into a semi-conscious state, from which three of them never rallied. There were no stimulants available to revive them as the small quantity of rum they had taken into the lifeboat had been issued on the first night out. There was nothing anyone could do. Their minds had become dull and vacant, their mouths were parched and their legs paralysed by the cold. It was snowing again, and hailstones beat against their faces.

At dusk, while it was still blowing a full gale, with a terrible sea running, they all began to suffer from delusions, apparently caused by the intense cold. The captain was at the steering oar, where he had been since they left the ship on the previous day. With the help of the sea anchor he had to keep the boat head to wind to ride the crashing waves but he was losing strength and it took all his willpower to keep up the desperate fight against the storm and his overwhelming tiredness. He could hardly keep his eyes open. 'Wake up, Robert, wake up,' Catherine shouted and slapped his face to keep him awake.

The first to succumb was Arnfors, the 21-year-old Finnish AB, who had been ill before leaving the ship. In his delirium and semi-conscious state he had rolled overboard, but was hauled in again and placed along the side of the boat. A little time later, at about 1900 on Tuesday night, he died. His death was followed quickly by that of Peter Subra, the cook and steward, and then of Nakarate, the Japanese cabin boy. Both men had worked below deck on the *Criccieth Castle* and were unused to the extreme exposure in mid-winter.

'It is the beginning of the end,' thought the captain. One of the seamen suggested throwing the bodies into the sea, but the captain said, 'No, give the poor fellows a chance to cool.' 'They cannot cool any more, captain,' he replied, 'They are absolutely frozen. It is the cold that has killed them.'

The lifeboat remained hove-to until later that night when the wind moderated slightly. A close-reefed sail was set and the boat again headed for the Falkland Islands as near as the wind would permit. Unfortunately not long after this she had to be hove-to once more as the wind rose again and a sea anchor was put out. At times oil was also used to reduce the waves in the vicinity of the boat.

The bodies were kept in the boat for five hours until about midnight. Their oilskins were removed and these were wrapped around Catherine and Bobby, who lay more dead than alive in the bottom of the boat, saturated in the icy water, which washed this way and that with the movement of the boat. Catherine cradled Bobby in her arms. He was unconscious, his flesh was deathly white and stone cold and he was badly frostbitten.

Roberts, the AB from Holyhead, assisted in heaving the bodies of his unfortunate comrades overboard and remarked, 'My word! What an easy way of dying – being frozen to death! I hope we shall all go like that, if we are to die.' Little did the poor fellow think, when he uttered those words, that he was doomed to suffer for six days longer and then die miserably in the bottom of the boat, with the icy-cold water washing over him.

'It's no good,' said one of the sailors, 'we might as well throw ourselves overboard now.'

'Don't talk like that,' Catherine said, 'Land can't be far away. We'll soon be rescued.' But inside her there was only emptiness and despair, except for the strange delusions.

Their delusions were becoming more frequent and a remarkable fact about these was that they all imagined they saw the same things at the same time. At first they thought they were all safe on their ship. The sailmaker remarked gravely, 'I am going to the galley for my coffee'; another man said he was going for a walk on deck to take the stiffness out of his legs. Then they thought they saw a long white building close to the starboard side of the boat. They thought they saw streets and houses. 'Look at that enormous cornfield,' Catherine shouted, pointing at the expanse of turbulent water stretching out to the horizon all around them. The others thought they saw corn blowing in the wind, too. Were they losing their minds?

One of the utensils which they had been using to bail out the water was a white enamel basin, about 12 inches in diameter. Presently the second mate, Frederick Sainsbury Lord, called out to the captain, 'Look at this basin, captain,' he said, 'What a monster, isn't it?' It happened that the captain had noticed it before he spoke, and it seemed to him to be some three feet in diameter instead of one; it appeared to his disordered imagination like an immense white tub. A little later Lord touched him and said, 'Look at that man's face!' pointing to one of the members of the crew. He looked, and it appeared to be three or four times its normal size. He drew Catherine's attention to it, and when she glanced up at her husband her face appeared the same, while she told him that his own had grown to four or five times its usual size. In the same way they imagined they saw a lot of other strange things. They could see the boat sailing up a wide road bordered on each side by white trees. Next they saw a big white-washed building in the middle of the road, and several of the crew called out to the captain to change course for fear of colliding with the building. Strangely these delusions only lasted for a few hours.

Robert stayed hour after hour holding the steering oar, and he was able to manoeuvre the boat using this. He was now barely conscious but realised that had he once let go of it for a moment the craft would have gone broadside onto the huge waves, which would have meant an instantaneous capsize and they would all have drowned. Later he wrote 'I really believe that I should have given up the attempt to reach land long before but for my wife and child. The desire to see them rescued induced me to fresh effort time after time. Under other circumstances I should have given up the ghost during the first two or three days.'

Then came the dreaded nightfall with its unbearable coldness and when Wednesday morning, July 17th, dawned they were, indeed, in a sad and sorry plight. The biscuits had become soaked with sea water and were like salty pulp. Their stomachs turned against the horrible stuff, as it only made them sick to eat it. The stock of water was also getting very low. Unfortunately one keg had been consumed during the first night – a fact the captain only discovered the next day. All the time he was steering the men were busy bailing out the water with any receptacle they could get hold of, and during these operations they had drunk the water. When Robert realised this he took the remaining keg and placed it at his feet. But one of the sailors had accidentally dropped some tobacco into this second keg and made it unpalatable for drinking. However, the consequence of this 'misfortune' was that the foul-tasting water lasted much longer than it would otherwise have done, and occasional sips were only taken of it when their thirst became unbearable. As already mentioned, they had also been forced to throw the case of tinned meat overboard to lighten their over-burdened craft in the heavy seas and so these sips of water were now their only sustenance, apart from some rain and snow that they caught with their open mouths. The spare oars were also thrown overboard and several other articles to further lighten the boat. It is possible that if the three men had not died the boat would have sunk under their weight.

Robert was still struggling at the steering oar, his hands frostbitten. All the crew, too, were in the same cruel predicament – their hands also frostbitten, black as ink in parts, swollen and wrapped like puddings against the cold and so numb and devoid of sufficient feeling that their fingers were of no use. The water was still rising in the boat and when they bailed out the water they had to hold the basin between their fists and wrists.

Chapter 8

OVERBOARD

Robert lost his grip on the steering oar and was washed clean overboard (WWM 1913)

A tremendous gale was still raging at 0800 on Wednesday 17th and there was a particularly heavy sea. Suddenly Robert lost his grip on the steering oar and he was washed clean overboard. The boat was unbalanced and rocked violently from side to side. Fortunately they had no headway at the time, as it was still hove-to, and was merely kept head-on to the sea with the steering oar. The sailmaker made a rush towards the oar immediately he saw what had happened; it was vital that the boat should be kept bows-on to the great waves that were running.

As for the captain, the next sea that came along nearly threw the boat on top of him. He managed to get one arm over the gunwale and the other through the life-line. But his hands were too badly frostbitten for him to be able to hang on by them, and at this critical moment they proved useless to him.

None of the crew stirred to help him into the boat; they were so numbed and exhausted that they could hardly move. Catherine and the second mate appealed to them to make the effort. 'Save him,' Catherine shouted hysterically. 'Save him. Save him or we'll all be drowned,' she pleaded and sobbed to the men. The captain knew he could not hold on much longer and was fast losing consciousness. With his heavy sea-boots and his wet clothing he felt as if he was being dragged down. The next instant he was being washed away in gigantic waves.

The crew still did not move and by herself Catherine could do nothing to save her husband from a terrible death. The sailmaker was aware of their predicament but he had to keep holding the steering oar in order to prevent the boat broaching and filling with water. In desperation Catherine found the pistol her husband had used to kill the pig just before they abandoned the ship. She could barely hold it and it would never have fired being totally water-logged and useless but nevertheless she threatened the crew. 'Help him, help him or I'll shoot you!' she cried. She prayed desperately that God would give the sailors the strength to save Robert's life and in terror she closed her eyes against the sight of her husband's struggle for life. Bobby's limp unconscious little body lay against her. Her own danger and even Bobby's receded from her mind as she leaned out over the side of the boat as if to will Robert back towards her. She had borne the misery of the past days as bravely as she could but she felt that without Robert there would be nothing. She never forgot that moment of horror.

Although it seemed like years, her eyes could not have been closed for more than a few seconds. When she opened them for a moment she was blinded by the stinging spray and her own tears, but a second later her sight was clear and she saw Robert's face in the water close to hers. A gigantic wave had thrown him back against the boat. With a sob of relief she tried to grab hold of him. Now the sailors rallied and by superhuman efforts they clutched hold of his clothes with teeth and arms and slowly managed to drag him back on board.

They placed him face downwards on the oars until he recovered from the shock. It was an hour before he regained consciousness. The second mate, young Frederick Sainsbury Lord, was pleased to see the captain safe, and remarked that it was a good omen, and that he was now sure they should reach land in safety. 'Thank God, you're saved!' was all Catherine could say to Robert. She wanted him to lie and rest for a while, but at about noon he insisted on returning to his post at the steering oar as if he knew that only action could keep hope alive.

'I'm going to get us back to land, somehow,' he said.

Here he remained in his sodden clothes and without any head covering. He had given up his oilskins and he tried to tie a handkerchief around his head but there was no one in the boat who could tie a knot under his chin, their hands were so frozen. He tried to hold the handkerchief on his head by gripping the ends between his teeth, but the wind blew it away. His clothes froze hard on his body.

Soon misfortune again befell them, for Kannegiesser, a 20-year-old German AB, died. Just before dusk they managed with great difficulty to slide his body over the side of the boat into the water. At about midnight of the same day, AB Joseph Smith died, and at daylight on Thursday 18th his, the fifth body, was consigned to the deep. Fortunately the weather had now moderated considerably and it kept fairly fine until that night. Then once again a tremendous gale began to blow from the northwest and with it a terrific sea which continued until some time in the afternoon of the following day, when the wind veered round suddenly to the southwest during a heavy squall. The wind blew much harder after shifting to the southwest, gusting at times to storm force. The sudden shift of wind was also responsible for a fearful cross sea which made it difficult for the little boat not to broach onto the waves and capsize. Finally some time during Friday night the gale moderated and by four o'clock on Saturday morning it had done so to such an extent that they were able for the first time in days to set a small jib on the craft.

They had no food, no water and their clothes were frozen on their bodies. Only Robert's fighting spirit gave hope in the face of such disaster, and Catherine's love and admiration for him gave her the strength to stave off the despair which had threatened to engulf her. Her greatest prayer was that her unborn child would live.

The lifeboat was now leaking so much they had to keep bailing the water out continuously. Each movement was a slow and painful operation and as they worked they became slower and slower. During those terrible days at sea their minds retreated into a kind of dream world where hardship was taken for granted and they were no longer afraid. Tragedy was accepted as something normal and never ending.

At dawn on Saturday 20th the wind dropped further and in the distance Catherine saw something that made her desert her dream world for reality once again. At first she could hardly believe her eyes, but when she looked again it was still there – a wavering low line on the horizon.

Chapter 9

FIRST LANDING

'Look,' she shouted, 'Land!' Those two words gave them fresh courage, and they thought their sufferings – they had now spent six days in the boat, practically without food – would soon be at an end. New life came to the sailors and with great excitement they pulled on their oars too. The mass ahead was so indistinct that Catherine began to wonder if her imagination was playing tricks, but slowly a craggy snow-covered island grew out of the sea and she could also see that Robert was excited. She watched her husband's face as she hugged Bobby to her with all her strength. Her husband turned towards her and smiled for the first time in days.

The lonely Beauchêne Island (Jim Elliott Collection)

'I think it's one of the Falkland Islands,' he said. Catherine did not care where it was; it could be anywhere. To her it was heaven on earth.

They took in the jib and waited for more daylight before attempting to land. But as the light revealed the outline, Robert discovered to his sorrow that it was the uninhabited Beauchêne Island. Beauchêne Island consists of rocky cliffs at both ends of the island, joined by a low lying isthmus. From a distance, the isthmus cannot be seen, and the two craggy ends give the appearance of two separate islands. 'It's a dead island,' said Robert, 'We couldn't survive here for more than a few days. They're uninhabited and about 30 miles south of the Falklands.' They were bitterly disappointed, needless to say, but set sail at once to make for the Falklands, and one can imagine their jubilation when, about noon, they sighted their goal.

At four o'clock in the afternoon they landed on the south coast of the East Falklands in a beautiful creek. Surely now, they thought, they would find succour and their trials would be over. They were all suffering terribly for want of water, their last keg being now exhausted, despite reducing the ration to less than half a cup a day. Some of the seamen were in a fearful condition, their swollen tongues hanging out nearly to their chins.

The ground where they landed was covered with snow, and they fell on their knees and commenced sucking it. Then they discovered a pool of brackish water, which they greedily drank. Rallying themselves before another long cold night set in, they gathered any spare clothing that remained in the boat, and with whatever twigs and grass they could find on the shore they were able to make a poor fire using matches that one of the crew had under his oilskins. Finally they fell down in the snow on the beach utterly exhausted. And there they remained all night.

At daylight on Sunday 21st the captain asked Osterstram (the carpenter), the strongest man in the party, to go with him inland to look for help, as he knew they could not hold out much longer, and none of the others were fit to travel. It was an exceedingly trying journey over the rocky ground, and more often than not they had to crawl over the rough boulders on their hands and

They found no salvation on this uninhabited part of the Falklands (R D Cadwalader)

knees, their feet being so numbed that they could not walk properly. After great physical sufferings they covered a few miles and it was made plain that misfortune was still dogging them. They realised they were on an uninhabited part of the Falklands, where no help could be found.

They returned to their companions about noon and reported the failure of their mission. Their disappointment was intense. Robert had left his wife and child in a very perilous condition and he would not have been at all surprised to have found them dead when he returned. Thank Heaven! They were still alive, but so badly frostbitten and ill that they were absolutely helpless. The sight of them wrung his heart for he could do nothing to alleviate their sufferings.

About two o'clock that afternoon they saw a small coaster

offshore so far away that only her mast and funnel were visible. The captain decided that they should try to catch her. At once they made preparations to embark, but they were very much hampered on account of their weak condition. One poor fellow, who was nearly dead, had to be lifted bodily into the boat using teeth and arms to do so. He appealed to be left to lie on the beach and die where he was. 'If your heart is not frozen and you have one spark of sympathy in you, you will let me die where I am, captain,' he moaned. Moving him, in his terrible plight, was simply torture, but the captain felt he could not let him remain behind. This man was Roberts, the poor fellow who had remarked that being frozen to death was an easy way of dying.

Over an hour elapsed between the time they first saw the vessel and when they were ready to put off. Night was fast approaching, and in addition the sky presented a wild and terrifying appearance, heralding the onset of another storm. The wind was now blowing off the land and they made good progress towards the distant ship. But fate was against them once more. After sailing right out to sea for about an hour they found it impossible to overtake the vessel and had to abandon the effort. Worn out with toil, hunger and thirst, they now began to feel the effects of the brackish water they had drunk and the snow they had eaten. Some of the men presented a terrifying appearance, foaming at the mouth like mad dogs.

The wind was increasing and the sea rapidly rising. They were from six to eight miles from land with the wind blowing off the shore. With the coaster disappearing they soon realised that they must try to get back to the land. They would have to use the oars instead of the sail for the return journey. When the captain ordered, 'Out oars and pull for the shore,' the men, with the little energy they had left, put out the oars, but failed to pull, having no feeling whatever in their abnormally huge hands.

However, they gallantly and pluckily did their best with their arms and wrists, being fully alive to the danger they were in, for the fast increasing wind threatened to drive them right out to sea where they would certainly die.

After some time it became clear they were making no headway – in fact they were not even holding their own. Soon the men became utterly exhausted; they could do no more. Dropping their oars, they fell back one by one, completely played out.

The little craft was now leaking badly as the result of having been buffeted about for so many days. All Sunday night they were shipping water and every moment they thought the boat would surely sink under them. They kept bailing all through the night, the poor crew holding the bailers as best they could with their wrists and teeth.

At about 0200 next morning, Monday 22nd, the sailmaker reported to the captain at the steering oar that Roberts, the man from Holyhead, was dead. This was the poor fellow who had appealed to be left to die on the beach.

It was now blowing a whole gale with squalls of storm force. The direction of the wind could not be ascertained as the glass of the compass had been broken to pieces through being washed about in the boat when she shipped a huge sea. They thought that the gale was still blowing from the land and none of them ever expected to see the shore again.

When morning started to dawn things did not improve; if anything they became worse and Robert felt certain this must be their last day. They had now been battling against fearful odds for eight days and he felt the end must be near – and the sooner it came the better. They had reached the limit of human resistance.

Then, as Robert glanced at his men, haggard and worn, their eyes protruding from their sockets and their tongues hanging out of their mouths, and at his poor wife and child lying helpless in the water in the bottom of the boat, a feeling swept over him. He realized that all of them were looking to him to pull them through. He made up his mind to fight to the last.

A deserted part of the Falkland Islands

Chapter 10

CAPE PEMBROKE

The wind, however, had providentially changed round during the night, and shortly after daylight they found to their intense delight that, instead of being out of sight of land, they were only three or four miles from it. They were, nevertheless, in a very critical situation, lying helpless in an open boat on a lee-shore – the coast of one of the rockiest regions in the world.

Every seaman who is acquainted with this locality knows full well how it can blow from the south here, and what the sea is like at such times. They were now faced with a terrible alternative; either to drift ashore before the raging gale onto the cruel rocks, or to set sail and try to weather a point of land about fifteen miles away, where they should get a little shelter from the wind and raging sea. The captain chose the latter course. The question now was how to put up the mast and set the sail. There was no time to lose as the lifeboat was quickly drifting towards the rocky shore. They were all so weak that they could not even move the mast, let alone set it up. Then the captain had the lucky thought to use the sprit of the sail as a mast, and this saved the situation. The boat's bow was turned towards the headland and she began to edge away from the dangerous rocky shore. When they were well under way it was decided to consign the body of the dead seaman in the bottom of the boat to the deep. They were so weak, having eaten hardly any food since they left the ship over a week previously, that it took them nearly an hour to slide the body over the side.

After sailing for some three or four hours they sighted the wireless poles of Stanley and at about noon they saw the lighthouse of Cape Pembroke.

The gale was still raging and finding a spot where they could land safely was proving difficult. It almost looked as if, at the last moment, after spending so many terrible days and nights enduring such hardships, they should be lost just as a haven of refuge came into sight. The coast here is very treacherous and studded with dangerous rocks, difficult enough for a fresh and healthy crew to manoeuvre a small boat among them in a calm sea, but they had no strength left and were absolutely at the mercy of the wind and waves.

The brave lighthouse-keepers took many risks (R D Cadwalader)

Presently they were driven close in shore. The captain ordered out the oars even though he knew the men had little strength left to manipulate them.

'Katie, Katie, we're almost there,' Robert said. Catherine had lost consciousness after they had all reboarded the boat to pursue the coaster. Now she tried to smile, but was too painfully cold to move her lips. She hugged little Bobby to her and his face was as cold as ice. He opened his eyes imploringly, 'Mummy, I want a glass of water,' he said. In eight days those were the first words he had spoken to her and Catherine told him gently he would have water as soon as they reached the island.

By this time they had been seen by the lighthouse-keepers at Cape Pembroke, Mr A W Sully and Herbert Price.

Robert had detected a small creek, known as the Gulch, at the base of the cliffs on which the lighthouse stood, and he steered for it. This was the spot where provisions for the lighthouse-men were landed, although Robert did not know this at the time. There was a big sea running and a particularly heavy swell. A big wave caught them and landed them upon a shoal where they were nearly swamped. Then a second wave carried them over this reef and deposited the boat right against the rock where the lighthouse-men land. At that moment one of the keepers jumped into the craft and with the help of the other keeper quickly made the lifeboat secure. Then they dragged the survivors out of the boat, one at a time, as the waves allowed.

The brave lighthouse-keepers worked hard, taking many personal risks to deposit everyone safely on the shore. Then they set about getting all the survivors to the lighthouse. First they took Catherine and then little Bobby. Everyone had to be carried as none of them could stand, let alone walk. Carrying the men with their garments saturated and frozen solid was extremely difficult. They had to carry them up the rocky steps and over the rough ground to the tower itself, and it took superhuman efforts by the keepers until at last they had put everyone in a big room, lit a blazing fire, and given them hot coffee to drink and bread and butter to eat. Most of them were drifting in and out of consciousness and could only take small sips. Slowly as their limbs began to thaw and the feeling returned they would learn the true meaning of agony.

Mr Sully telephoned to Stanley, advising the authorities there of the rescue and the sad plight of the survivors. The

Governor at once dispatched a doctor. Dr Browne was formerly the medical officer to the Derry Workhouse before he went to live on the Falklands. With a guide to show the way they left Stanley on horseback to travel the four and a half miles across the rough boulders, against a tremendous wind, to get to the lighthouse.

Meanwhile, a boat's crew of Government men with another crew from the Falkland Islands Company along with the Chief Constable and a captain embarked on the Government launch *Penguin*. They took Nurse Whieldon from the Victoria Cottage Home hospital with a plentiful supply of warm clothing and blankets. The frozen survivors were to be collected and taken back to Stanley.

When the Governor heard that the second boat of crew from the *Criccieth Castle* had gone missing he arranged for Captain Hansen of the steamer *Harpun* to get together a crew of fourteen volunteers willing to set off on what would probably be an abortive mission. By working all night putting on coal and fitting her engines they were able to set off at 0800 on Tuesday 23rd. Not very surprisingly they did not manage to find the longboat.

The Governor made sure that the owners of the *Criccieth Castle* in Britain were informed about the shipwreck and the survivors. In the previous year, 1911, Guglielmo Marconi had installed a wireless telegraphy station on the Falkland Islands and this enabled telegrams to be sent to Montevideo in Uruguay 1,500 miles away.

At the lighthouse the doctor and his helpers had to cut away the survivors' clothing and boots as these had become stuck fast to their bodies, and some of the men were so frostbitten that their flesh came away with the fragments of clothing.

As soon as they had been dressed in warm clothing and wrapped in blankets, the eleven survivors were carried down to the launch, and at half-past eleven that night they were put to bed in the Victoria Cottage Home at Stanley. Of the 24 people who had to abandon the *Criccieth Castle*, eleven were still alive and of

Nurse Whieldon and Mr Scully, the lighthouse-keeper (WWM 1913)

these, two more were to die from their ordeal.

When Catherine was almost asleep that first night in Stanley the matron came into her room. From the look on the matron's face she knew there was something wrong. Her heart sank as she was told that Bobby's feet had swollen to such an extent that they had burst through his boots, and when the doctor had cut away the leather he had found that it would be necessary to amputate the little boy's feet. The doctor feared blood-poisoning and he would carry out the operation the next day. 'Your son's feet are badly frostbitten and the poison can't be allowed to spread. I'm afraid we'll have to amputate his legs in the morning.'

For the first time since the shipwreck Catherine burst into tears. Had she not already lived through enough without this? She lay awake sobbing, the doctor's words echoing in her ears, praying and asking herself this question over and over again.

In the morning the matron came in. She was smiling and Catherine knew that her prayers had been answered again. 'Is he all right?' she asked. 'Yes,' said the matron, 'the circulation came back into his legs during the night. They'll be all right. But it will be some time before he'll be able to walk.'

Catherine breathed a sigh of relief. All she wanted now was to know that Robert was going to recover too. Like them all he had suffered terribly and had collapsed on arrival at the hospital. He was unconscious for another four days. When at last Catherine was allowed to see him he clasped her hand and said, 'You were wonderful, Katie.' Robert was deeply concerned about his wife and their unborn child. She smiled happily but felt unworthy of his praise. She knew that it was his strength and courage which had saved them, his fighting spirit and determination that enabled him to man the steering oar day after day, keeping their small craft from disappearing under the waves.

Two of the men with frozen limbs were in such a terrible state that the doctor considered it would be useless to carry out any amputation as their chance of survival was negligible. And unfortunately, despite the care and attention that was given them, they died in the hospital. Frederick Sainsbury Lord, the young apprentice who had served on the *Criccieth Castle* for four years before being promoted to second mate in Callao, died aged 20 on 3rd August. The reason given for his death was 'Primary: Frostbite, Secondary: Tetanus'. Juan Cecchi from Ancona, Italy, died aged 19 on 7th August. He had joined the ship as an OS in Callao. Both men are buried in Stanley Cemetery near the water's edge in 'Block I' plots '748' and '749'.

The others, suffering terribly, remained in the hospital until they were fit enough to travel. Many of them had to have some fingers and toes removed to prevent blood-poisoning as a result of frostbite and William Summers and G Osterstram lost all their toes.

Catherine lay between the sheets of her hospital bed, marvelling that she had been saved and that she still had both Robert and Bobby. How had they managed to pull through when six strong men in the lifeboat had died? Perhaps the love between Catherine and Robert had given them that extra strength of will which made all the difference. The doctors told Catherine later that her pregnancy had probably increased her strength. It was years later that she read that in some cases people can go into a sort of suspended state after long periods of extreme cold – in the same way that animals go into hibernation. In this way they use minimal energy and survive without drink or food. It is possible that this is how Bobby survived. He was wrapped in oil skins and being small would have been below the sides of the boat and thus sheltered from the worst of the wind. Some of the time at least he would have been held by Catherine and this may have kept him out of the water at the bottom of the boat. He was unconscious for most of the eight days, his body closed down. Miraculously he survived.

Victoria Cottage Home (courtesy of the Falkland Islands Museum & National Trust Cobb Collection)

Chapter 11

RETURN TO BRITAIN

After a period of convalescence and the arrival of the next mail steamer, the *Oropesa*, at Stanley, six of the survivors were able to leave for England on August 6th, but three still remained in hospital. They had to carry Catherine and Bobby on board, and Catherine remained in bed for another three weeks. Robert was able to walk to the steamer on crutches, being unable even then to fully use his feet and legs. It was not until they reached Liverpool that Bobby was able to put his feet to the ground and try to walk.

Before he left, Robert wrote this letter to Dr Browne and it was published in The Falkland Islands Magazine in September 1912:

Cottage Home, August 6th, 1912
Dr W Browne,
Stanley

My Very Dear Sir,

I really do not know how to thank you for the constant attention we have received since we have been under your care. I would take this opportunity of asking you to convey to His Excellency the Governor and to all the people of Stanley our appreciation for their many kindnesses to us.

I write this on behalf of self and family and all the crew.
With many thanks for all you have done,
I remain,
Yours very sincerely,
Robert Thomas, Master

The survivors who landed in Liverpool spoke with tears in their eyes of the kindness and humanity with which they had been treated by the inhabitants of the Falkland Islands, from Governor Allardyce downwards. With Robert, Catherine and Bobby were three ABs from Finland, Samuel Numiquiner and Kusta Laine who had joined the ship at Leghorn in March the year before and H Kinnunen who joined the ship in Callao. All these men were in their twenties. Their pay for the voyage was £18.10s.2$^{1}/_{2}$d for Numiquiner, £13.9s.10d for Laine and £8.0s.11d for Kinnunen.

Newspapers reported the arrival of these survivors the next day. On September 4th 1912 the Guardian newspaper ran this story:

LOSS OF A WELSH SHIP - TERRIBLE OPEN BOAT VOYAGE TO THE FALKLANDS

The Pacific liner Oropesa, which arrived in Liverpool yesterday, brought Captain Robert Thomas, his wife and child and three sailors of the Criccieth Castle, which was abandoned in a waterlogged condition on a homeward voyage from Peru with a cargo of guano.

One of the crew relates a terrible experience. He says there was a lifeboat and big dinghy aboard, and in the lifeboat the captain, his wife and son, and 15 others embarked, while the mate and eight others took the dinghy. The second boat has never since been heard of. The boats lost sight of one another in the dark, although they endeavoured to keep in company. They were 150 miles from the Falkland Islands, and had some tinned food, biscuits and a little water. A heavy sea was running, which nearly swamped the boat. On the second day a Finn, a French cook, and a Japanese died, and on the third day a German and an Englishman. On the morning of the fourth day they found a Welshman dead, and him also they sent over the side. By this time nearly all were frostbitten. The captain had been washed out of the boat, but managed to scramble back again. All suffered agonies. The food and water gave out. When in an exhausted condition they sighted a large sailing ship two miles off, but failed to attract her attention. After seven days they reached an outlying island of the Falklands, and lit a fire and enjoyed a drink of melted snow. To find an inhabited island they put to sea again, and were blown out of sight of land. Eventually they reached

Stanley Harbour. Two of the men died in the hospital there, and others have been left behind with a hope that they may recover.

The Criccieth Castle was a sailing ship of 1,877 tons, built in 1887, and owned by the Criccieth Castle Company, of Criccieth, Carnarvon.

On 30th September the three survivors who had remained in the hospital at Stanley now arrived in Liverpool on board the *Oravia*. All of them must have regretted joining the ship in Callao six months before. The first of the three men was G Osterstram, the 41-year-old ship's carpenter from Arendal, Sweden, who as the fittest man had been chosen to go with the captain to explore the landfall that proved to be uninhabited; his final pay was £12.0s.3d. The second man was E M Westerberg, the 45-year-old sailmaker from Mariaham, Finland whose quick-wittedness had saved the day when he took control of the steering oar when the captain had been washed overboard. His payout was £14.6s.8d. And finally there was William Summers, the 21-year-old AB from Dundee, who had persevered so nobly to attempt to bail the rotten wheat from the bottom of the hold despite the appalling fumes. He received £7.17s.2d. The men's story appeared on 1st October in the Daily Mail when they ran this article:

ADRIFT OFF CAPE HORN

A terrible account of sufferings at sea was given by the survivors of the Liverpool sailing ship Criccieth Castle, which was abandoned when on a voyage from Lobos, in Peru, to the United Kingdom for orders. The ship carried a crew of twenty-five, including Captain Robert Thomas, who was accompanied by his wife and little son, aged four. She rounded Cape Horn safely in spite of rough weather, but later on the ship was subjected to a terrible battering by heavy seas. The rudder shaft snapped and the sternpost was dragged away.

Suffered fearful privations

The ship began to make water rapidly, and the crew had to take to the boats. The mate and eight men put off in the dinghy and the remainder in the lifeboat. They kept company from three o'clock in the afternoon until eleven at night, when the dinghy was lost to sight and was never seen again. Each boat had been provisioned with tinned meat, bags of biscuits and a small quantity of water.

Those in the lifeboat suffered fearful privations, owing to the severity of the Arctic weather. On the second day of their exposure two of the sailors, a Jap and a Finn, and the cook, a Frenchman, died. Most of those in the boat had already been frostbitten, and before the dead men were thrown overboard their clothes were taken in order to provide protection for the others.

The captain was washed out of the boat, but on the following wave he succeeded in grasping the gunwale and was dragged on board by his wife. On the third day two more of the crew, an Englishman and a German, succumbed, and at daybreak another man, a Welshman, was found frozen to death.

All this time Captain Thomas was steering for the Falkland Islands, and on the seventh day the boat, with great difficulty, reached an islet on the northern part of the group. Those in the boat were completely exhausted, but they managed to scramble ashore, and warmed their perished limbs as well as they could by a fire made with withered alfalfa grass, and refreshed themselves with a drink made of melted snow.

Treated with kindness and humanity

Finding no other sustenance on the islet they put to sea again, but were blown off their course by another terrible storm. Eventually they sighted the northernmost lighthouse in the islands, and were at last brought to Port Stanley, where all the survivors had to be carried ashore and taken to hospital. Their clothing and boots, which were frozen to their bodies, had to be cut away, and some of the men were so frostbitten that their flesh came away with the fragments of clothing. The second officer and another man died in the hospital. Amputation of the men's limbs would, in the opinion of the doctors, have been useless, so terrible was the state of the patients.

On the arrival of the next mail steamer at Port Stanley six of the survivors were able to leave for England, but four still remained in hospital. The survivors who landed in Liverpool spoke with tears in their eyes of the kindness and humanity with which they had been treated by the inhabitants of the Islands, from Governor Allardyce downwards.

A Board of Trade inquiry into the loss of the *Criccieth Castle* was held in Liverpool on 16th, 17th, 18th, 22nd, 23rd, and 24th days of October, 1912. A full copy of this report (The Board of Trade Inquiry into the Abandonment of the *Criccieth Castle*: No. 7561) is given in Appendix VIII of this book. The captain was represented by Mr L S Holmes of Miller, Taylor, and Holmes. The main focus of the inquiry seems to have been to establish the blame for the not clearing out of the hold after the unloading of the wheat in Callao and before the loading of the guano from the Islas Ballestas. Expert evidence was given during the trial as to the effect of guano mixed with salt water from leakage, and of the manner in which that might affect the working of the pumps. It was the captain's contention that the non-working of the pumps was due almost entirely to this cause, but the Court were unanimously of the opinion that it was the grain in the bilge that prevented their proper working.

The result of the inquiry was published in The Times on 26th December 1912:

The Loss of The Ship Criccieth Castle. Judgment of The Court.

Judgment was given at Liverpool yesterday in the Board of Trade inquiry respecting the loss of the Liverpool sailing ship Criccieth Castle, which foundered off the Falkland Islands in July while bound from Ballistas, Peru, for Antwerp with guano. The inquiry extended over six days before Mr STUART DEACON, stipendiary, and three nautical assessors: Rear-Admiral Ernest Fleet, Captain John Taylor, and Captain John H Walker. In giving judgment the STIPENDIARY said that the Court found the vessel was in good order and in seaworthy condition before the last voyage. The bilges were properly cleaned, with the exception of a section amidships in which wheat, part of a previous cargo, had been left, with the result that water entering the ship was prevented from reaching the pump well. The immediate cause of the casualty was the breaking of the rudder stock occasioned by heavy sea causing damage and consequent leakage. A contributory cause was the fact that the chief mate, although he had received specific instructions from the captain, omitted to have the bilges in the vicinity of the pump well properly cleaned of the wheat in Ballistas. The result of such omission was the condition preventing water reaching the pump well. The pumps, therefore, when resorted to were useless. The fact that the wheat had been left in some bilges was made known to the captain by the first mate seven or eight days after the vessel had left Ballistas with a cargo of guano, and the captain caused efforts to be made on two successive days to have the wheat cleared away; but the men were unable to do the work owing to the unbearable stench caused by the guano or wheat, or both. The Court felt that the captain might have caused further efforts to be made to clear the wheat away. It was evident that he was alive to possible danger from the wheat to his pumps. Although the Court was not prepared to say that the captain in not making such further efforts was guilty of actual default, the fact that the pumps were not earlier resorted to after the accident was considered by the Court to be in some degree due to the captain's previous knowledge of the presence of wheat in the bilges! It was evident that such earlier resort, even if it were in fact possible, would have been of no avail. The Stipendiary proceeded: 'Having said so much, the Court has the satisfaction of further saying that the captain, after the abandonment of the ship had become a necessity, did all in his power to secure the safety of his crew and the preservation of the lives of those who survive to-day may be regarded as due to his vigilance and efforts during the terrible ordeal in the lifeboat.' In regard to the longboat, which went down with the first mate and six hands, the Court expressed the opinion that had it been provided with a sail possibly it would have safely reached the Falkland Isles and the lives of those on board would have been saved.

A further report into the loss of the ship was given in the Mercantile Marine Service Association Reporter Volume 38 1913, pp 38-43, entitled 'Notes On Recent Wreck Inquiries'. A full copy of this report is given in Appendix IX.

The fate of the lifeboat left on the Falklands may be found in Appendix XII and there is more information about Cape Pembroke's lighthouses in Appendix XIII.

At last they returned home to Llangybi and their house, Gorsannedd

Chapter 12

THE FOLLOWING YEARS

At last Catherine, Robert and Bobby were able to return home to Llangybi where Catherine spent a few weeks in bed and Robert hobbled around on crutches.

Robert was deeply concerned about Catherine and their unborn child, but a few weeks later on 23rd November 1912 she gave birth to a baby girl who was strong, healthy and completely normal. They were overjoyed, for this seemed to be the most wonderful miracle of all. They named her Mercy Malvina, 'Mercy' because they had been spared and 'Malvina' because this is the Spanish name for the Falkland Islands where they landed.

It was wonderful to be back among the lovely green hills and countryside of Wales again. Robert was not yet well enough to work, so they stayed at home together doing all the things they had not been able to do before – going for long walks, or just sitting by the fire talking and playing with the children. Gradually they learned to live with all their memories and to put the past behind them, although it was reported in an article in the Carnarvon Herald on September 13th 1912 that the little lad 'cannot bear to hear mention of his sufferings during that memorable voyage.' Every day Catherine spent hours helping Bobby to walk again. He used to look out of the window and see the other children passing by in the lane, longing to join them. He wanted to run on the beach and play like other youngsters but it was a year before he recovered the full use of his legs. Soon there was not a boy in Llangybi who could beat him at running across the fields. Mercy also grew up into a lively child. They were all happy and nothing it seemed could destroy their contentment.

The strain and exposure told on Robert's health, and for some months he was incapacitated from service. Then he joined an oil tanker, but was not yet in a fit condition to stand the rigours of another voyage. His health again broke down, compelling him to rest for 18 months. During this time he wrote up their incredible story for an article in The Wide World Magazine. Interestingly this article was reproduced in The Advertiser newspaper in Adelaide, South Australia on Tuesday 22 July 1913.

In 1914 the world was becoming engulfed in what was later

Robert Thomas became a Lieutenant of the Royal Naval Reserve

to be called the First World War. Robert took a Commission as Lieutenant in the Royal Naval Reserve and was made Commanding Officer of *HMS Kelvin*, a mine-sweeper. In this capacity he rendered very able service in the dangerous waters and arduous conditions of the North Sea. On one occasion they were instrumental in salvaging a seaplane whose engines had failed. They also rescued several sailors who were in danger of drowning after the sinking of their vessel by a German mine. Robert, as the captain, received many grateful letters of appreciation.

Catherine was now pregnant with their third child and their second son was born on 20th April 1917. They named him 'Kelvin' after the ship that Robert commanded.

However, their joy was short-lived as on July 3rd 1917 Robert was hurt in a mine explosion. Nevertheless he remained on duty but died four days later on July 7th. It was a terrible blow to Catherine but she felt thankful for the years of happiness they had won together. Also they had had the chance to prove their love in the face of the severest test and Catherine knew it would live on in her heart.

Robert's death was widely mourned for he had won friends in all parts of the world by his happy, cheerful and genial disposition. The Commander-in-Charge at Harwich wrote to Catherine 'It would be impossible for me to speak too highly of the very real and manly service of your late husband during his long and dangerous service at Harwich.' (See Appendix X for the Roll of Honour and Appendix XI for a funeral notice found in the Pritchard family Bible).

From their Majesties the King and Queen came a gracious message of sympathy, whilst my Lords Commissioners of the Admiralty wrote: 'That Lieutenant Thomas has shown great zeal and courage in the performance of his dangerous duties.'

Mourning photograph of Catherine, Bobby, baby Kelvin and Mercy (Sylvia Swainson Collection)

From the Commander of Auxiliary Patrols at Harwich came the following: 'He was a most gallant officer beloved by everybody, untiring in zeal and devotion to duty, and of the many officers I have had here, none carried out orders more explicitly and faithfully than he did. His loss is a very grievous one to the nation besides yourself... Had he lived he would have undoubtedly received the Distinguished Service Order, which he had earned by his gallantry at all times.'

In warm appreciation, a brother officer wrote of Lieutenant Thomas as: 'A grand fellow... always so keen and willing and capable at this terrible work of mine sweeping.'

Robert's body was brought home and his funeral at Capel Helyg, Llangybi, was an impressive ceremony. A naval party from his own ship were present. Mr William George, brother of the Prime Minister, addressed the naval escort and paid warm tribute to the noble character and happy disposition of Lieutenant Thomas. Also among the people at the funeral were Dr Livingstone Davies, one of the Criccieth GPs and Mr Burnell, the headmaster at Criccieth Primary School since 1880 who was also the Chairman of the Council and Honorary Secretary of the Criccieth RNLI, plus many other prominent Criccieth businessmen and master mariners.

Little Bobby grew up into a strong young man who as his father had predicted took to the sea. He was 5 feet $4^1/_2$ inches tall with grey eyes and light brown hair. At 16 years of age he was on the *Piako* and served on at least three other ships before joining the *Trafford Hall*.

In September 1933 he was a quartermaster on the *SS Kioto* in Antwerp. One night, Bobby, with some of the crew, was returning to the ship after being ashore when the steering oar of their gig fell into the water. Immediately Bobby dived into the black waters of the harbour to recover the oar but he failed to find it and his clothing grew heavy. In no time at all he was dragged below the surface. Eventually he was pulled from the water and taken to the ship where a doctor pronounced him dead; the cause of death was 'accidentally drowned'. It was another terrible blow for his mother, Catherine, to bear for the rest of her life. On October 12th 1933 the North Wales Observer ran this story: *'Harbour Tragedy - Criccieth Man Drowned at Antwerp. News has been received by Mrs Thomas, widow of Captain Thomas, Gorsannedd, Llangybi, South Caernarvonshire, of the drowning at Antwerp of her son, Robert Thomas (25), quartermaster of the steamship Kioto, of the Hall Line, Liverpool.'*

'It appears that Thomas was returning to the ship from shore with some officers in the boat. Thomas was sculling when the oar accidentally slipped. He jumped into the harbour to retrieve the oar, but was drowned. The body was recovered. When he was four years of age Thomas and his mother were passengers on the ship Criccieth Castle, of which Captain Thomas was master. The ship was lost in a storm off Cape Horn, and he and his parents and the crew were adrift for a week in an open boat before being rescued.'

Bobby was also buried in the cemetery of the chapel at Llangybi. His name was added to the large memorial with these words, 'and also their eldest son, Robert, drowned at Antwerp 27th September 1933, buried here October 1933 aged 25 years. Peace Perfect Peace.'

Catherine continued to live at Gorsannedd in Llangybi. Mercy Malvina attended Bangor Girls' School and she left there on 19th December 1929 to go to the Dispensing College in southwest London to train to become a dispenser. On 2nd January 1934 when she was 21 she married Geoffrey Wallis, a ship's officer. This marriage did not work out and she returned to North Wales to live with Catherine until her marriage to Dr T H Rhys of Pwllheli. Together they had two daughters, Linda and Sylvia. Mercy died on 25th May 1966 aged 54 and her daughter Linda died in 1998 at the age of 42. Both are buried at the chapel cemetery in Llangybi. Sylvia has two children, Simon Richard

Swainson born in January 1969 and Katherine Elizabeth Swainson born in October 1970.

Kelvin, Robert and Catherine's third child, grew up in Llangybi. He attended the primary school in Llangybi and later Pwllheli Grammar School. He studied accountancy at a college near Bangor, and worked in London as an accountant and auditor. In 1945 he married Nina Spencer and together they had one daughter named Fiona. In 1961 Kelvin was taken ill with a respiratory problem and he died on 17th March 1961 at the age of only 43 years, when Fiona was eleven years old. Nina and Fiona moved to Carmarthen to be near Nina's sister.

For over 50 years Catherine's two unmarried sisters, Annie and Maggie Pritchard, had run the family shop in Llangybi until they died in 1960. The shop was taken over by Myfanwy Jones from Pencaenewydd, who ran the shop from 1961 to 1987. In 2010 Sylvia and I visited Myfanwy who was delighted to find a home for a box of large old books that had been left in the shop when she took it over. Amongst the books was the Pritchard family Bible with a family tree (see Appendix V).

In 1962, after a stroke, Catherine went to live with Mercy and her husband and their two young daughters in Pwllheli. She died on 15th May 1970 in a home at Porthmadog; she was 85 years of age and had outlived all her children.

A few years before she died she said, 'Now my greatest joy is to sit around the fireside with my grandchildren, telling them about the fascinating places I visited across the ocean, and the fun and adventure of my life with Robert on the *Criccieth Castle.* I shall never forget her massive white sails billowing out in the wind and the great love they symbolize for me.'

The Criccieth Castle by William Godfrey (Sylvia Swainson Collection)

Appendix I

Glossary

AB	able-bodied seaman
after-hold	the cargo compartment in the stern of a ship
afterhatch	an opening in the deck above a hold in the stern of a ship
amidships	located in the middle part of a ship
barque	a ship with three (or more) masts with square sails on all the masts except the sternmost that has sails that are set along the line of the keel rather than perpendicular to it
beam (on the)	when the ship is sailing at a right angle to the wind is usually the fastest point of sail
bilges	the lowest inner part of a ship's hull
bill of lading	a document supplied to the exporter by the shipping company that is transporting the goods to their foreign destination, listing, item by item, the goods being shipped
block	a wooden or metal case in which one or more pulleys are placed to gain mechanical advantage
bow	the front of a ship
braces	lines or cables attached to the ends of each yard and used to pivot (brace) the yards around the mast at different angles to the fore-and-aft line of the ship to make the most of the wind
bulkhead	a wall within the hull of a ship
burlap	a cloth made from jute and also known as hessian
capstan	a vertical-axled rotating machine developed for use on sailing ships to apply force to ropes, cables, and hawsers
chain sheet	the attachment for controlling the bottom corners

	of some sails was by chain rather than rope
chocks	a heavy fitting of metal or wood with two jaws curving inward, through which a rope or cable may be run
clew up (verb)	raise the lower corners of a square sail by means of clew lines ie take up the sails
coaming	a raised section of deck plating around an opening, such as a hatch also they provide a frame onto which to fit a hatch cover
consignee	the receiver of delivered goods
consignor	one who delivers goods to a ship or other carrier
crojack	the lowermost sail on the mizzen-mast
davit tackle	part of a small crane on a ship that is used to raise and lower small boats, such as lifeboats
discharge certificate	from 1854 certificates of discharge were issued to crew members at the end of each voyage. They were normally required before a seaman was signed on to a new ship
forecastle	the upper deck of a sailing ship forward of the foremast, or the forward part of a ship with the sailors' living quarters
forehatch	an opening in the deck above a hold in the forward part of a ship
foremast	the first mast, or the mast fore of the main-mast. Sections: fore-mast lower — fore topmast — fore topgallant mast
forepeak	the section of the hold of a ship that is within the angle made by the bow and is used for trimming or for storage of cargo
freeboard	the height of a ship's deck above water level
gaff	a spar attached to the mast and used to extend the upper edge of a fore-and-aft sail

gaff-end	the outside end of a gaff
gig	a long, light ship's boat sometimes reserved for use by the ship's captain
gunwale	the upper edge of the side of a boat
guys	ropes used to steady, guide or secure something
hatch	an opening in the deck of a ship, such as, above the hold
hatchway	a covered opening in a ship’s deck through which cargo can be loaded or access made to a lower deck
head pump	the pump used to flush the toilet (or head) projecting from the bows
heel of the mast	the lowest part of a mast
hold	the cargo compartment of a ship
horseshoe plate	a plate around a ship’s rudder stock that is shaped like a horseshoe and designed to prevent water from entering the rudder trunk
hove-to	a boat is headed directly into the wind so that it is not sailing forward
hull down	the situation where the upper part of a vessel or vehicle is visible, but the hull is not visible
keelson	a girder fastened above and parallel to the keel of a ship for additional strength
lame duck	a person or company that is in trouble and needs help
lanyard	a rope that ties something off
leading wind	a wind at right angles to a ship and hence a good sailing wind
lower topsails	a square sail rigged above the course (or lowermost) sail and below the topgallant sail where carried

main truck (see truck)

mainmast	the tallest mast, usually located near the centre of the ship
mizzen mast	the third mast immediately behind (aft) of the mainmast and typically shorter than the fore-mast
mast	a mast may have three sections to it. The top section is the royal or topgallant mast, the middle section is the topmast and the bottom section is the lower mast
OS	ordinary seaman
poop deck	the short sternmost raised deck of a vessel
riding light	a light in the rigging of an anchored ship
royals	a small sail flown immediately above the topgallant
rudder chains	one of the loose chains which fasten the rudder to the quarters to prevent its loss in case it gets unshipped, and for operating it in case the tiller or the wheel is broken
rudderstock	a vertical post at the forward edge of a rudder that enables the rudder to pivot
running gear	the rigging used to manipulate sails, spars etc in order to control the movement of the ship
sails	see the illustration on page 33 for the names of the sails on the *Criccieth Castle*
serving board	part of apparatus to make a tight cover to protect the rigging
sheet	a rope used to control the setting of a sail in relation to the direction of the wind
shoreside	on shore
Southern Cross	a well known constellation of stars visible in the Southern Hemisphere
spar	a stout rounded usually wood or metal piece

	perpendicular to the mast used to support rigging
sprit	a spar that is attached to the mast and bisects the face of the sail with its other end attached to the peak of the sail
staves	narrow strips of wood that form part of the sides of a wooden boat
steering gear	all parts of the mechanism used for steering a ship
stern	the back part of the ship
sternpost	the principal upright post at the stern of a vessel used to support the rudder
storm staysail	small triangular sails used primarily in storm conditions
tallyman	one who checks and keeps a record of receipt of goods
thwartships	across the ship cf. the thwarts on which rowers sit
tiller	a lever attached to a rudder stock of a boat that provides leverage for the helmsman to turn the rudder directly by pulling or pushing it
tot	a small measure of spirits
truck	the wooden bun-shaped cap at the top of a mast
washports	an opening in the rail along the deck to allow water to drain, also called freeing ports
yard	the horizontal spars used with square sails
yardarm	the two tapering outer ends of a ship's yard
yellow fever	a very infectious disease spread by mosquitoes. The fever, nausea and pain were in some cases followed by death

Appendix II

Some Sources and Further Reading

Robert Cadwalader's website http://freespace.virgin.net/r.cadwalader/
'Gwraig y Capten' by Aled Eames 1984
'I Married The Sea' by Jane Deveson, Woman's Own magazine March 16th 1963
'Kicking Canvas' By A A Bestic 1959
'Last of the Windjammers' (Two Volumes) by Basil Lubbock 1927
'Learning The Ropes: A Seaman's Apprenticeship' by Julie Stone
'Maid of Athens and Criccieth Castle' by Jim Elliott, The Falkland Islands Journal 2000 pp 98-108
'Reminiscences of the Criccieth Castle - February, 1907 to March, 1908' by Edmund B Howard in Sea Breezes Volume 19 1934 pp 9-12
'Schooner Captain' by Hugh Shaw 1972
'Sail Ho!' by Sir James Bisset 1961
'Seafaring Under Sail' by Basil Greenhill 1981
'Ships and Seamen of Gwynedd' by Aled Eames 1976
'The Great Grain Race' by Eric Newby 1956
'The Last of the Cape Horners' by Claude Lombard Aubry Woollard 1967
'The Merchant Schooners' by Basil Greenhill 1988
'The Nitrate Clippers' by Basil Lubbock 1966
'The War with Cape Horn', 'By Way of Cape Horn', 'The Set of the Sails' and other books and booklets by Alan Villiers
'The Wreck Of The Criccieth Castle' by Robert Thomas, The Wide World Magazine 1913 pp 322-332
'The Wreck of the Criccieth Castle' by Jocelyn Greenway, Maritime Wales 2009 Number 30 pp 46-54
'Twilight of Welsh Sail' by Aled Eames 1984
'Two Years Before The Mast' by Richard Henry Dana 1840
'Typhoon' and other novels by Joseph Conrad
'Ventures in Sail' by Aled Eames 1987

Appendix III

Two Articles by Jocelyn Greenway

ABOARD A GIRLS' TRAINING SHIP

(An article about the *English Rose II* by Jocelyn M Greenway from *The Christian Science Monitor*, September 10th 1956)

English Rose II lay on a quiet mooring in Poole Harbour when we visited her. A black, two-masted sailing ship, she was built in 1900 of teak, and, she is now owned by Commander Claude Woollard, who runs her as a girls' training ship. He believes she is the only one of her kind in the world.

Commander Woollard has trained over 2,300 girls since he started this venture during the war, and with his girl crews he has crossed the channel to France many times. He is so well known at Honfleur, the beautiful and unspoiled little port at the entrance to the River Seine, that they literally put out the red carpet for him when he puts in there. He has been made a freeman of the town, too.

On one occasion he took his ship up the River Seine to Paris, and such was the cooperation of the lock keepers that they passed the ship through so quickly that she arrived in Paris a whole day early, to the dismay of the authorities, who were arranging a great reception for her crew. However, the reception duly took place, the girls were fêted and invited to numerous gatherings, and all left with the most rosy pictures of the hospitality offered to them in Paris.

The most recent adventure of *English Rose* was taking part in the World's Sail Training Ships Race to Lisbon. Commander Woollard and the girls sailed her around to Dartmouth, the starting point for the race, where a week's regatta was held for the ships taking part. Quite a fleet of sailing vessels were gathered from all over the world.

English Rose, the only one with a girl crew, was not able to complete the course as the girls could only be away for a fortnight's holiday, but she competed in the small boat races at Dartmouth, and crossed the starting line with the rest, heading out into the channel in a choppy sea. After encountering fog and light winds, the race was won by the British ketch *Moyana*, while *English Rose* made her way up channel to Poole once more to pick up a new crew.

When we saw the ship, only the commander, his chief officer, Ann Rhodes, who is an ex-sea-ranger and a former trainee of his, were on board, with one French girl member of the crew. Eight more were arriving that evening. We were shown over the ship by the chief officer. There were ten berths, with a possible eleventh, folding wash basins in some of the cabins, locker space for each girl, and a roomy galley. There is quite a library in the main cabin, for those who want to read.

The crew members are divided into two watches as soon as they arrive, the starboard watch having their bunks all along the starboard side of the ship, and the port watch all along the port side. A full training programme is drawn up with all duties allocated between the two watches.

The French girl had baked some cakes, and my husband and I, and our young daughter, Jill, were invited to go below. While we were enjoying it, Commander Woollard regaled us with tales of rounding Cape Horn in the three-masted sailing ship *Penrhyn Castle*, in which he served as a midshipman and junior officer for over six years. He is a real mariner, and channel and coastal cruising can hold few terrors for one who has seen his ship literally disappear beneath a great wave in the Southern Seas. They thought she had gone, he told us, when very slowly, she rose, throwing off the tons of water from her decks.

I feel sure the commander could have told many more interesting tales, but his crew was due to arrive in the evening, and there were finishing touches to be put to *English Rose* before they arrived. We had enjoyed our visit so much. Jill was almost signed on to join the Training scheme as soon as she reaches the age of 14.

We feel that Commander Woollard is doing a great work in making available to girls the character training, skills, and joys of the sea, and we wished that there were more ships of this kind available to them.

CAPE HORN SAILORS GET TOGETHER

(An article by Jocelyn M Greenway published in *The Christian Science Monitor,* Saturday July 19th 1958)

Have you ever seen the Greybeards of Cape Horn? Have you ever lived in quarters awash with salt water for weeks on end, and struggled with stiff, wet canvas in a gale, up on the yards 150 feet above deck? There are many living today who have done all these things, and are banding together in the International Association of Master Mariners, otherwise known as Cape Horners.

This association was founded in 1937 at St Malo, home of the deep sea sailors of Brittany, France, and full membership is open to all seamen of any nationality who hold a master's certificate of competency and who have rounded Cape Horn in a sailing vessel, either before the mast, or as an apprentice, midshipman, mate, or master. The membership is now over 1,000 and it is increasing rapidly. Those who have rounded Cape Horn in command of sailing vessels are designated as Albatross and others as Mollyhawks. Others who have rounded the Cape, but do not hold a master's certificate, and women who have made the voyage, are eligible to join as associate members.

Commander Woollard is the founder of the recently formed British section of this association, and some 80 members have already joined. Among these are several women. I have been reading some of the letters which the commander has received from women applicants for membership. They are from the wives and daughters of sailing ship masters, and although the letters are mostly brief, they do give a glimpse of life on long voyages under sail. A letter from a woman associate states that she made the journey round the Horn when she was ten years old in the company of her father, who was master of the ship. She has vivid recollections of being bound to the rigging on the poop deck to view the heavy seas in comparative safety. The crews of the old sailing ships were usually of different nationalities. They had no time for factions, but were united for the job in hand, namely, bringing the ship into port.

There are now branches in Australia, Denmark, Germany, and Belgium, and it is hoped that there will soon be one in the United States. A three days' congress takes place annually at one of the large seaports. Last year it was held at Antwerp, and this year it will be held at St Malo from June 13th to 16th. Members from many parts of the world are expected to attend. No doubt many tales of life on the turbulent grey seas off the lonely Cape will be exchanged, fulfilling the aim of the association, which reads in part, 'to perpetuate the ties of comradeship and friendship which bind all Cape Horners throughout the world'.

Appendix IV

The Thomas Family Tree

Robert Thomas (Robert's grandfather) 1815 – 1850 Master Mariner (died in Caernarfon on board *Cyfartha*) married Ann. They had six children:

1) Evan Thomas (1838 – 1889) Master Mariner
2) Henry Thomas born 1841 Master Mariner
3) Jane Thomas born 1844 married Richard Jones
4) Ann Thomas born 1846 married Eos Eifion (bard)
5) Elinor (Elin) Thomas born 1847 married Hugh Jones and they had eleven children including Charles (Charlie) born 1872, who was killed at sea and buried in Talcahuano, and Jane Thomas born 1885, the mother of Roberta who died in 2011 and Glenys. Glenys had four children, Jane born 1954 (two daughters - Mari born 1987 and Ellen born 1989), Ann born 1956 (two sons and one daughter - Ifan born 1985, Catrin born 1988 and Huw born 1989), Elin born 1960 and died in 1982, and Trystan born 1961.
6) Robert Thomas (Robert's father) 1849 – 1881 Master Mariner (died of fever on board *Cygnet* in Rio Grande do Sul, South America) married Anne born 1855.

Robert Thomas (Robert's father) 1849 – 1881 and Anne had three children

1) Robert Thomas 1879 – 1917 married Catherine Pritchard (1885 – 1970) in 1907
2) Anne Thomas born 1877
3) Catherine Thomas born 1880

Robert Thomas (1879 – 1917) and Catherine had three children

1) Robert Thomas (Bobby) 1908 – 1933 survived the ordeal in 1912 at the age of four and drowned at Antwerp aged 25

years.

2) Mercy Thomas 1912 – 1966 married Geoffrey Wallis in 1934. Some years later she married Dr Rhys from Pwllheli and they had two daughters, Linda and Sylvia. Linda Ann was born 8th January 1948, she married Michael Leslie Allford and she died on 5th February 1992. Her sister Sylvia has two children, Simon Richard Swainson born in January 1969 and Katherine Elizabeth Swainson born in October 1970.

3) Kelvin Thomas 1917 – 1961 married Nina Spencer and they had one daughter, Fiona.

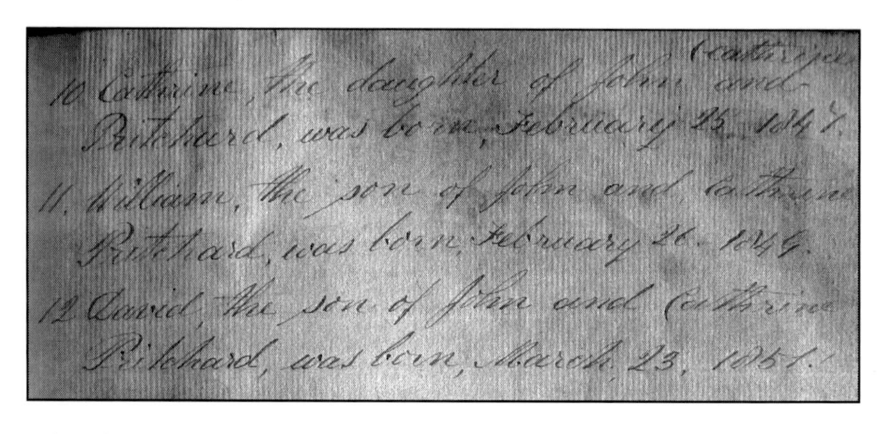

10 Catherine, the daughter of John and Catherine
Pritchard, was born, February 25, 1847.
11. William, the son of John and Catherine
Pritchard, was born, February 26. 1849.
12 David, the son of John and Catherine
Pritchard, was born, March 23, 1851.

This shows John and Catherine Pritchard's children, 10 to 12, from the hand written lists in their Bible

Appendix V

The Pritchard Family Tree

This tree is compiled from handwritten sheets found in the Pritchard Bible.

John Rowlands married Jane Evans and they had a daughter Ellinor Rowlands.

John Pritchard married Ellinor Rowlands on 3rd July 1827 in Llangefni, Anglesey.

They had these children:

1. John born October 4th 1828
2. John born November 1829
3. Jane born April 7th 1831
4. Ellinor born ? 31st 1833
5. Ann born January 16th 1835
6. John born April 5th 1837
7. Margaret born March 6th 1839
8. Lidia born March 10th 1841
9. William born September 15th 1843

Ellinor Pritchard died June 6th 1844 at the age of 35??

John Pritchard then married Catherine (surname unknown) and together they had:

10. Catherine born February 25th 1847
11. William born February 26th 1849
12. David born March 23rd 1851

The 11th child William was the father of Catherine Thomas (née Pritchard)

William (11. above) married Ellen Evans on 3rd July 1874 in the Welsh Presbyterian Church, Toxteth Park, Liverpool. They had these children:

1) David born in about 1879

2) Catherine born in about 1873 who died in childhood
3) William born in about 1883
4) Catherine born in 1885. She married Captain Robert Thomas in Cardiff in 1907
5) Ann born in 1887
6) Margret born in 1886
7) Hugh born in 1891 (headmaster of Llanystumdwy School and father of the artist Gwilym Pritichard who was born in 1931)

The Silverdale before she was renamed the Criccieth Castle. There are six sails on each mast. The number was reduced to five so that fewer men were needed to crew the ship

Appendix VI

Notes on the *Criccieth Castle*

When the *Criccieth Castle* was built in Workington by Williamson and Company she was called the *Silverdale*. Williamson & Son was established at Harrington, Cumbria in about 1839 by the Williamson family. Their business was building brigs, four-masted barques, barges, lighters and other small ships. In 1880 the business moved to Workington in Cumbria and the yard closed in 1939.

The *Silverdale* was an iron-hulled ship of 1877 registered tons with dimensions of 263 feet 9 inches in length by 39 feet wide by 23 feet 7 inches deep with a 47 feet poop deck and a 26 feet forecastle. She was a three-masted sailing ship with six sails on each mast. She was launched on 10th March 1887. In October 1889 she was sold to Robert Thomas and Company of Criccieth and Liverpool for the sum of £18,500.

Robert Thomas (unrelated to Captain Robert Thomas) was a former Nefyn schoolteacher whose ships were well known throughout the world. He renamed the *Silverdale* the *Criccieth Castle* after Criccieth Castle in Wales. A single ship company was set up called the Ship Criccieth Castle Company which initially had its registered office at 5 Bryntirion Terrace, Criccieth before moving to 49 High Street, Criccieth. Later, in 1899, the office moved to 26 Chapel Street, Liverpool.

Robert Thomas had the number of sails on each mast reduced from six to five. He probably changed the upper and lower topgallant sails into just one topgallant on each of the three masts. The purpose of this was to reduce the work on the ship and hence the number of crew members. Profit margins were tight and any means for saving money would have been undertaken.

Appendix VII

Crew Agreements

Crew agreements or crew lists contain a wealth of information and many are held by the Maritime History Archive, Memorial University of Newfoundland, St Johns from where copies can be bought. Each agreement refers to one ship's voyage and they are catalogued by the year the voyage ended.

In the 18th century crew agreements were required onboard UK ships to collect a levy from the crew's wages for a relief fund for sailors and as a record for all men serving on a particular ship. The 1835 Merchant Shipping Act required all ships to have a crew agreement as it was intended that a central register would be kept of all seamen who might be called on to support the Royal Navy. The crew agreement must be signed by each crew member upon joining and leaving a ship.

Most crew agreements contain the following information: description of the ship and its owners, name of the ship's master/captain, voyage's port of commencement, voyage's destination and port of termination, rules or laws to be observed during the voyage, particulars of each member of the crew including name (signature), age, place of birth, previous ship, place and date of signing, capacity (AB, carpenter, 2nd mate etc), when expected on board, pay for the journey, and crew's addresses, also particulars of discharge (eg end of voyage, desertion, sickness, death, never joined etc) and ports visited with endorsements by British Consuls or other nominated personnel.

Crew Agreement of the *Criccieth Castle* 1911 to 1912

The fact that the 1911 to 1912 crew agreement for the *Criccieth Castle* survived the shipwreck and arrived in the Falklands, still legible, means that it would have been wrapped in oiled cloth and carried in the lifeboat. The agreement shows the fines for various offences that might be committed on board ship; for example the fine for Drunkenness (First Offence) was Five Shillings, and for

Second and Subsequent Offences the fine was Ten Shillings; the fine for Striking of Assaulting Any Person on Board or Belonging to the Ship was Five Shillings.

Each crew member had to sign on themselves and it is interesting to note that most of them had very neat handwriting, and that many different nationalities were represented.

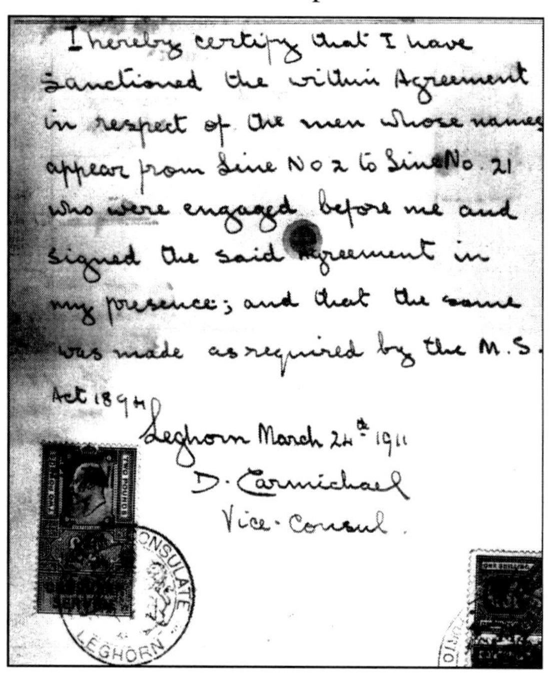

I hereby certify that I have sanctioned the within Agreement in respect of the men whose names appear from Line No 2 to Line No. 21 who were engaged before me and signed the said Agreement in my presence; and that the same was made as required by the M.S. Act 1894

Leghorn March 24th 1911

D. Carmichael
Vice-Consul.

CONSULATE
LEGHORN

The authorisation of the new crew agreement by the Vice-Consul at Leghorn

The British Consuls or a port official had to sign and stamp the agreements at any ports where crew members left or joined the ships. At the start of the 1911 voyage of the *Criccieth Castle* from Leghorn in Italy the Vice-Consul wrote: ‘I hereby certify that I have sanctioned the within Agreement in respect of the men whose names appear from Line No 2 to Line No 21 who were engaged before me and signed the said Agreement in my presence; and that the same was made as required by the MS Act

1894 Leghorn March 24th 1911 (signed) D Carmichael, Vice-Consul'.

Before leaving the Falkland Islands the Agreement had to be signed by a representative from the Falkland Islands Shipping Office. W A Thompson wrote and signed the following on 30th August 1912: 'I hereby certify that the within mention seamen Nos 1, 9, 18, 21, 40, 41, 43 & 50 have been discharged before me on the ground of shipwreck and that Nos 42, 48 & 55 have died and Nos 15, 44 to 47, 49, 51 to 54 and 56 have been reported as missing.' (Note: Seaman No 2 was mistakenly left off the list of those reported missing.)

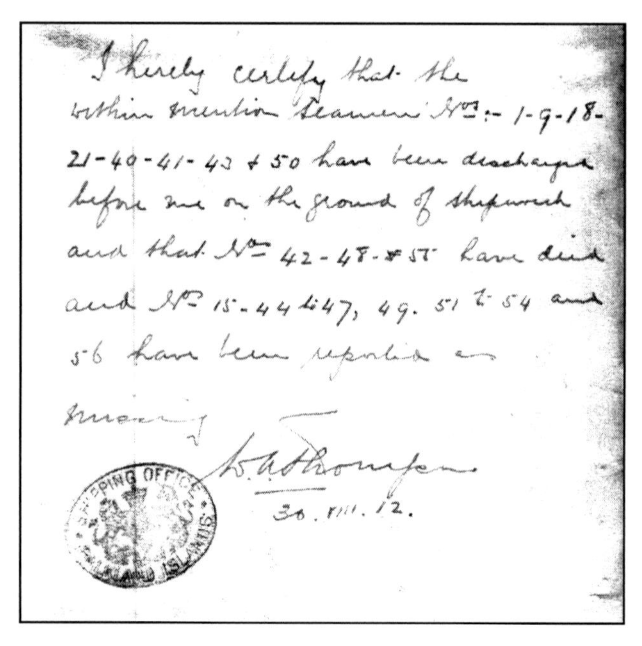

I hereby certify that the within mention Seamen Nos:- 1-9-18-21-40-41-43 & 50 have been discharged before me on the ground of shipwreck and that Nos 42-48-&55 have died and Nos 15-44 to 47, 49. 51 to 54 and 56 have been reported as missing

W A Thompson
30. VIII. 12.

SHIPPING OFFICE ... FALKLAND ISLANDS

The crew sign off, including deceased and missing members, by the Falkland Islands Shipping Office representative

The four apprentices were signed on in a special section of the crew agreement called the 'Account of Apprentices on Board'. It shows the first one, Frederick Sainsbury Lord, was born in 1892 in Sunderland and he began his apprenticeship (indenture) on

April 6th 1908. After four years as an apprentice Lord finished his indenture on 5th April 1912 when the ship was in Callao, and Page 8 of the agreement shows him being signed on as the second mate on 8th April 1912. Page 9 shows that Lord died in Stanley on August 3rd 1912 with the cause of death, according to a copy of a death certificate, 'Primary: Frostbite and Secondary: Tetanus'.

The apprentice, Fred Upham Hellyer from Hull, began his indenture on May 19th 1908. During the 1911 to 1912 voyage, having completed his four years as an unpaid apprentice, he was promoted to third mate on May 19th 1912. Hellyer was placed in the ill-fated longboat and on line 56 on Page 9 under the Release coloumn is written, 'Reported Missing'.

The two other apprentices, Maurice Victor Millar from Wolverhampton and Harold Read from Halifax, must have decided to try their luck in Australia. They both deserted in Port Pirie on the 23rd and 24th November 1911 respectively. It would be interesting to find out what became of these two young men, perhaps they turned their backs on the sea and settled in South Australia?

ACCOUNT OF APPRENTICES ON BOARD.

Christian and Surnames of the Apprentices at full length. 1.	Year of Birth. 2.	Nationality* (If British, state birthplace.) 3.	Registry of Indenture. Date of 4.	Port of 5.	Date of Joining subsequent to commencement of this Agreement. 6.	Date, Place, and Cause of leaving this ship, or of Death. If the Apprentice remains it should be stated. To be filled up by the Master. Date. 7.	Place. 8.	Cause. 9.
Frederick Sainsbury Lord	1892	Sunderland	April 6th 1908	L'pool	April 6th 1911	5/4/1912	Callao	Having terminated apprenticeship [illegible]
Maurice Victor Millar	1891	Wolverhampton	June 5th 1909	Sunderland	June 5th 1911	23/11/11	Pirie	b.a.l. 1/c received Deserted
Fred Upham Hellyer	1892	Hull	May 19th 1908	L'pool	May 19th 1911		See line 56	[illegible]
Harold Read	1894	Halifax (Yorks)	23 May 1909	Sunderland	21 May 11	24/11/11	Pirie	b.a.l. 1/c received Deserted

Of the four apprentices who were signed on for the 1911 to 1912 voyage of the Criccieth Castle, two deserted in Port Pirie

4

Name of

PARTICULARS

Reference No.	SIGNATURES OF CREW.	Age.	*Nationality (If British, state birthplace).	(1) Port of Engagement Address, and (2) Home Address. N.B.—Both to be inserted. The Home Address is the one to which communications should be made in the event of the death of the Seaman.	Ship in which he last served, and Year of Discharge therefrom. Year.	State Name and Official No. or Port she belonged to.	Date and Place of Signing this Agreement. Date.	Place.
1	2	3	4	5	6	7	8	
1	Master to sign first Robt. Thomas	32	Criccieth	(1) Gorsanedd (2) Llanystumdwy Chwilog		Same	23/3/11	Leghorn
2	William A. Gale	26	Brit	(1) St Olaves (2) Ramsey I. O. M	1911	Same	23/3/11	Leghorn
3	Arthur Andrews	25	Manchester	(1) C/o John Andrews (2) [illegible]	"	"	"	"
4	Jas. Campbell	28	Greenock	(1) Sailors Home (2) Greenock	"	Cheyenne	"	"
5	[illegible]	18	Dane	(1) Holmbadsgade (2) Copenhagen	"	Foreign	"	"
6	Ingford Böckmann	22	Norway	(1) Schelldrop St 30 (2) Christiania	"	"	"	"
7	[illegible] Pasquale	22	Italy	(1) Reggio Calabria (2) Catona	"	[illegible]	"	"
8	Costantinos + Raly	24	Greek	(1) (2) Constantinople	"	Foreign	"	"
9	[illegible]	26	Russia	(1) [illegible] (2) Finland	"	"	"	"
10	[illegible]	[illegible]	Do	(1) [illegible] (2) Finland	"	"	"	"
11	[illegible]	22	Austria	(1) Zara (2) Austria	"	[illegible]	"	"
12	Costa + Vlahakis	21	Greek	(1) Chios (2)	"	Foreign	"	"
13	Pandelis + [illegible]	22	"	(1) Smyrna (2)	"	"	"	"
14	Costantinos [illegible]	22	"	(1) Constantinople (2)	"	"	"	"
15	[illegible]	52	London	(1) 124 [illegible] Rd (2) Lower Clapton	"	[illegible] Castle L'pool	"	"
16	Charles McIntee	20	[illegible]	(1) 12 [illegible] St Belfast (2) Ireland	"	Foreign	"	"
17	Evan Jones	64	[illegible]	(1) 12 Bank Place (2) Portmadoc	1910	[illegible] L'pool	"	"
18	C. Thomas	24	Llangybi	(1) Bryn Gwalia (2) Carnarvon	1911	Same	"	"
19	Wm. [illegible]	36	Cork	(1) 28 [illegible] St (2) Cork	1911	Foreign	23/3/11	"
20	Guiglermo Rossetti	27	Spanish	(1) 3 Vico Mele (2) Genova	"	do	"	"

* If a British Subject, state Town or Country of Birth, and if born in a foreign

† The capacities of Engineers not employed on the Propelling Engines and Boilers should be described here and in the Certificate of Discharge as Engine Drivers, Donkeymen, Refrigerating Engineers,

‡ If the advance of wages is not conditional on going to sea, the

§ If any Member of the Crew enters His Majesty's Service, the Name of the King's Ship into which he enters is to be stated under the head of "*Cause of leaving*

Page 4 of the 1911/1912 crew agreement – Robert Thomas is the first crew member to sign on and Catherine was the eighteenth

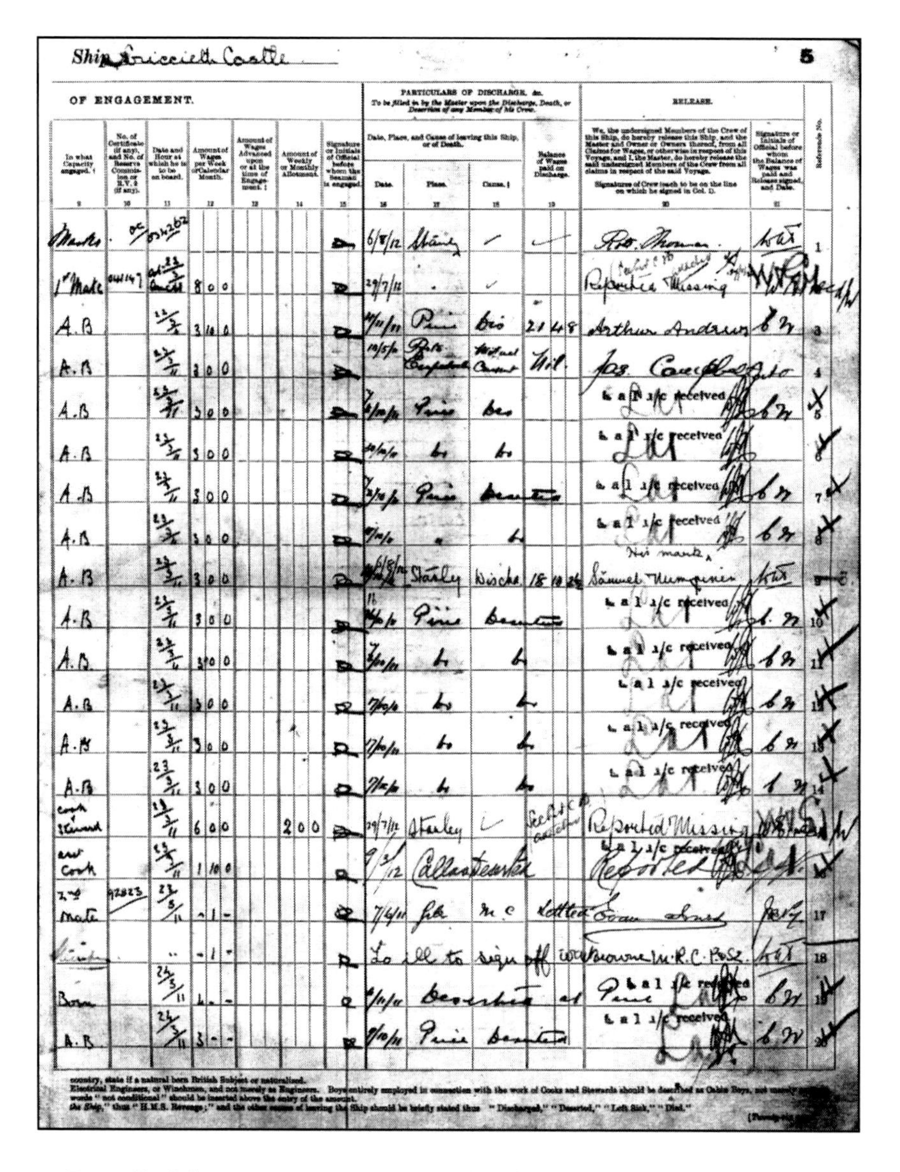

Ship Criccieth Castle — 5

OF ENGAGEMENT. — PARTICULARS OF DISCHARGE, &c. To be filled in by the Master upon the Discharge, Death, or Desertion of any Member of his Crew. — RELEASE.

In what Capacity engaged (9)	No. of Certificate (if any), and No. of Reserve Commission or R.V.3 (if any) (10)	Date and Hour at which he is to be on board (11)	Amount of Wages per Week or Calendar Month (12)	Amount of Wages Advanced upon or at the time of Engagement (13)	Amount of Weekly or Monthly Allotment (14)	Signature or Initials of Official before whom the Seaman is engaged (15)	Date (16)	Place (17)	Cause (18)	Balance of Wages paid on Discharge (19)	We, the undersigned Members of the Crew of this Ship, do hereby release this Ship, and the Master and Owner or Owners thereof, from all Claims for Wages, or otherwise in respect of this Voyage, and I, the Master, do hereby release the said undersigned Members of the Crew from all claims in respect of the said Voyage. Signatures of Crew (each to be on the line on which he signed in Col. D.) (20)	Signature or Initials of Official before whom the Balance of Wages was paid and Release signed, and Date (21)	Reference No.
Master	OC 034262					[illegible]	6/8/12	Stanley	✓	✓	Robt. Thomas	WET	1
1st Mate	041147	23/3/11	8 0 0			[illegible]	29/7/11	"	✓		Reported Missing	[illegible]	2
A.B		23/3/11	3 10 0			[illegible]	4/10/11	Pirie	Dis	21 4 8	Arthur Andrews	[illegible]	3
A.B		23/3/11	3 0 0			[illegible]	10/5/12	Port Stanley	Mutual Consent	Nil	Jas. Campbell	[illegible]	4
A.B		23/3/11	3 0 0			[illegible]	7/10/11	Pirie	Des		L a 1 1/c received	[illegible]	5
A.B		23/3/11	3 0 0			[illegible]	10/10/11	do	do		L a 1 1/c received		6
A.B		23/3/11	3 0 0			[illegible]	7/10/11	Pirie	Deserted		L a 1 1/c received	[illegible]	7
A.B		23/3/11	3 0 0			[illegible]	9/10/11	"	do		L a 1 1/c received	[illegible]	8
A.B		23/3/11	3 0 0			[illegible]	6/8/12	Stanley	Discharged	18 10 2	His mark Samuel Humphries	WET	9
A.B		23/3/11	3 0 0			[illegible]	11/10/11	Pirie	Deserted		L a 1 1/c received	[illegible]	10
A.B		23/3/11	3 0 0			[illegible]	7/10/11	do	do		L a 1 1/c received	[illegible]	11
A.B		23/3/11	3 0 0			[illegible]	7/10/11	do	do		L a 1 1/c received	[illegible]	12
A.B		23/3/11	3 0 0			[illegible]	7/10/11	do	do		L a 1 1/c received	[illegible]	13
A.B		23/3/11	3 0 0			[illegible]	7/10/11	do	do		L a 1 1/c received	[illegible]	14
Cook & Steward		23/3/11	6 0 0		2 0 0	[illegible]	29/7/11	Stanley	✓	[illegible]	Reported Missing	[illegible]	15
Asst Cook		23/3/11	1 10 0			[illegible]	9/3/12	Callao	Deserted		L a 1 1/c received Reported	[illegible]	16
2nd Mate	92823	23/3/11	-/1/-			[illegible]	7/4/11	[illegible]	M.C.	Letter	Evan Jones	[illegible]	17
[illegible]		..	-/1/-			[illegible]	Too ill to sign off			[illegible]	Browne [illegible]	WET	18
Boy		23/3/11	1 - -			[illegible]	4/10/11	Deserted at Pirie			L a 1 1/c received	[illegible]	19
A.B		23/3/11	3 - -			[illegible]	9/10/11	Pirie	Deserted		L a 1 1/c received	[illegible]	20

country, state if a natural born British Subject or naturalised.
Electrical Engineers, or Winchmen, and not merely as Engineers. Boys entirely employed in connection with the work of Cooks and Stewards should be described as Cabin Boys, not merely
words "not conditional" should be inserted above the entry of the amount.
the Ship," thus "H.M.S. Revenge;" and the other causes of leaving the Ship should be briefly stated thus "Discharged," "Deserted," "Left Sick," "Died."

Page 5 of the crew agreement – under the Discharge column note the number of crew who deserted in Port Pirie, and also note Catherine was too ill to sign off in the Falklands

6 Name of

PARTICULARS

Reference No.	SIGNATURES OF CREW.	Age.	*Nationality (If British, state birthplace).	(1) Port of Engagement Address, and (2) Home Address. N.B.—Both to be inserted. The Home Address is the one to which communications should be made in the event of the death of the Seaman.	Ship in which he last served, and Year of Discharge therefrom. Year.	State Name and Official No. or Port she belonged to.	Date and Place of Signing this Agreement. Date.	Place.
1	1	2	3	4	5	6	7	8
21	Kusta Laine	25	Russia	(1) (2) Raumo	1911	Foreign	24/3/11	Leghorn
22	Wm R Whyte	28	Lerwick	(1) 122 Provincial (2) Glasgow Scotland	1911	Cosmessi	21/4/11	Port Empedocle
23	James Parry	26	B/head	(1) Gila (2) 17 Weston St. B/head	1911	Dovenby	7/8/11	Gila
24	X M. Sullivan	35	Br	(1) (2) Dungarvan Ireland	"	Loch	4/11/11	Paris
25	H Wingaton	38	"	(1) (2) London	Cambrian Peer	"	do
26	T. Ruthowski	32	German	(1) (2) Dantzic	"	Oltenia	"	do
27	J. Evans	27	Br	(1) (2) Port Madoc	"	Pres	"	do
28	E.R.J. Carr	32	"	(1) (2) Mt Gambier	"	Reverie	"	do
29	W Scource	21	"	(1) (2) Bowden		First	"	do
30	C.A. Fuller	16	"	(1) (2) London - Eastwood (Parkside)		do	"	do
31	Johan Riis	25	Norway	(1) (2) Fredrikstad		Anglo Norm	9/11/11	"
32	Wm Kennedy	"	Br	(1) (2) Manchester		Loch Garry	"	"
33	Olof Lundberg	31	Sweden	(1) (2) Stockholm		Holbeuten	"	do
34	C.W. Winstol	28	USA	(1) (2) Bowen USA		do	"	do
35	~~C.W.O. Winstol~~ Thomas Foss	34	Norway	(1) (2) Bergen		do	"	do
36	S Starling	20	Br	(1) (2) Blakeney Norfolk		Ormsary	"	do
37	W Owen	19	"	(1) (2) Criccieth Wales		Milverton	"	do
38	R D Jones	21	"	(1) (2) Carnarvon		Peregrine	"	do
39	~~Otto Schroeder~~	30	German	(1) (2) Holland		Antelope	7/10/11	do
40	G Westram / DIS. A NOT PRODUCED / J G [illegible]	41	Arendal Sweden	(1) Constitucion #82 (2) Arendal, Sweden	1912	Foreign	30/3/12	Callao

* If a British Subject, state Town or Country of Birth, and if born in a foreign

† The capacities of Engineers not employed on the Propelling Engines and Boilers should be described here and in the Certificate of Discharge as Engine Drivers, Donkeymen, Refrigerating Engineers,

‡ If the advance of wages is not conditional on going to sea, the

§ If any Member of the Crew enters His Majesty's Service, the Name of the King's Ship into which he enters is to be stated under the head of "Cause of leaving

Page 6 of the crew agreement shows the columns with Age, Nationality, Date and Place of Signing On etc

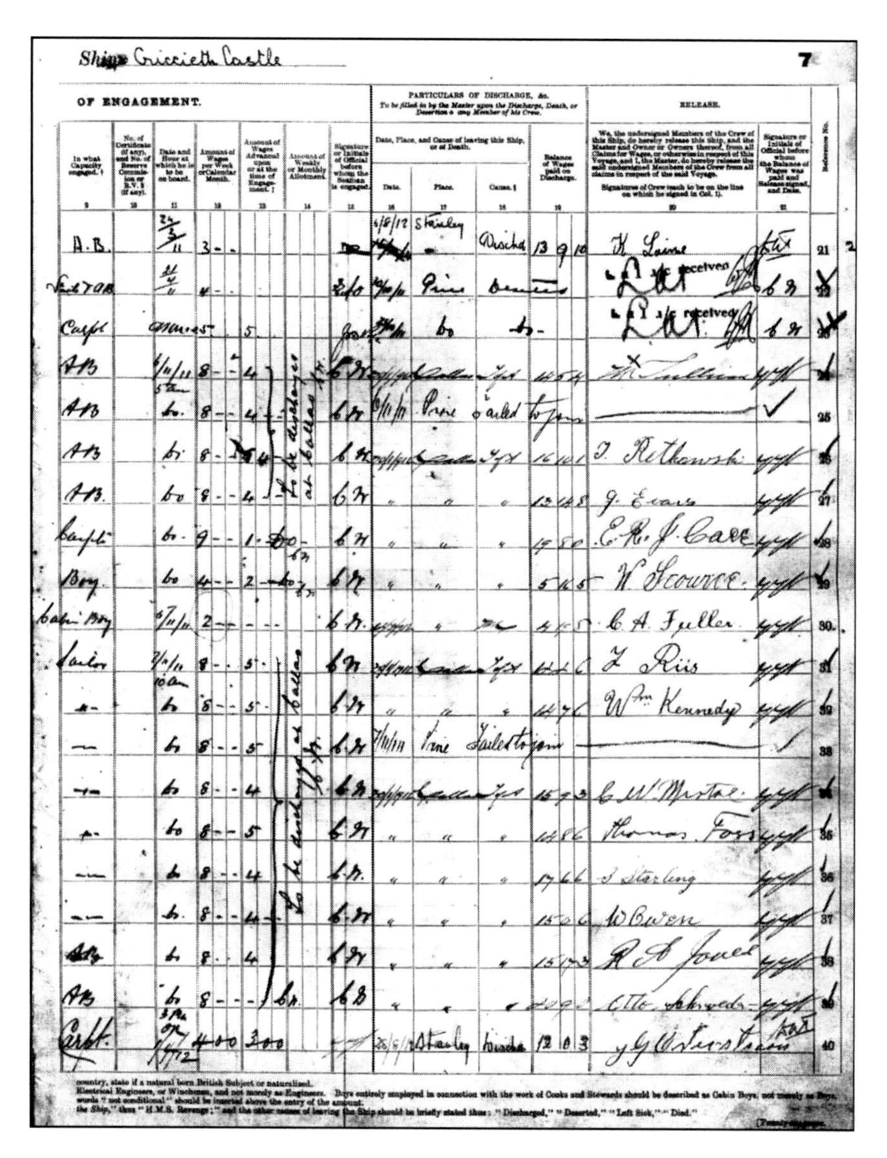

Ship Criccieth Castle 7

OF ENGAGEMENT.

PARTICULARS OF DISCHARGE, &c.

RELEASE.

Page 7 of the crew agreement shows many of the crew left the ship in Callao under their Terms of Agreement and the amounts they were paid

8 Names of

PARTICULARS

Reference No.	Signatures of Crew	Age	*Nationality (If British, state birthplace)	(1) Port of Engagement Address, and (2) Home Address	Ship in which he last served, and Year of Discharge therefrom: Year	State Name and Official No. or Port she belonged to	Date and Place of Signing this Agreement: Date	Place
41	E. M. Westerberg	45	Mariehamn	(1) On board (2) Mariehamn, Finland	1912	Foreign	30/3/12	Callao
42	J. Arnfors	21	Finland	(1) On board (2) Rauma, Finland	1912	do.	"	"
43	H. Kinnunen	24	Viborg	(1) On board (2) Viborg, Finland	1912	do.	"	"
44	T. Wilson	43	Jersey	(1) [illegible] (2) [illegible] St, Kimberley	1912	[illegible]	"	"
45	E. Kannegiesser	20	Stettin	(1) [illegible] (2) [illegible], Stettin	1912	Foreign	"	"
46	E. [illegible]	23	Sweden	(1) Miller 33 (2) [illegible], Sweden	1912	do.	"	"
47	Nakayama [illegible]	25	[illegible]	(1) [illegible] (2) [illegible] Japan	1912	do.	"	"
48	[illegible]	19	Ancona	(1) No 43 [illegible] (2) do.	1912	do.	1/4/12	"
49	Geo. Powell	32	Cardiff	(1) [illegible] (2) [illegible], Cardiff	1912	do	1/4/12	"
50	William Summers	21	Dundee	(1) Miller 381 (2) Balmoral [illegible]	1912	do.	"	"
51	J. Roberts	38	Anglesea	(1) Miller 381 (2) [illegible] St Harwich	1912	do	"	"
52	J. Martin	39	London	(1) Miller 381 (2) Blundell St [illegible] London	1912	do.	"	"
53	T. Barker	56	[illegible]	(1) Miller 381 (2) 15 [illegible]	1912	do	"	"
54	Joseph Smith	49	Liverpool	(1) Miller 381 (2) 4 Walnut St, Liverpool	1912	do.	"	"
55	Frederick [illegible]	20	[illegible]	(1) on board (2) [illegible]		[illegible]	[illegible]	"
56	Fred E. Hellyer	20	Hull	(1) on board (2) 18 [illegible]		"	19/5/12	
57								
58								
59								
60								

* If a British Subject, state Town or Country of Birth, and if born in a foreign [illegible]

† The capacities of Engineers not employed on the Propelling Engines and Boilers should be described here and in the Certificate of Discharge as Engine Drivers, Donkeymen, Refrigerating Engineers, [illegible]

‡ If the advance of wages is not conditional on going to sea, the [illegible]

‖ If any Member of the Crew enters His Majesty's Service, the Name of the King's Ship into which he enters is to be stated under the head of "Cause of leaving [illegible]"

Page 8 of the crew agreement shows the last two crew to be signed on were the former apprentices who now became second and third mates

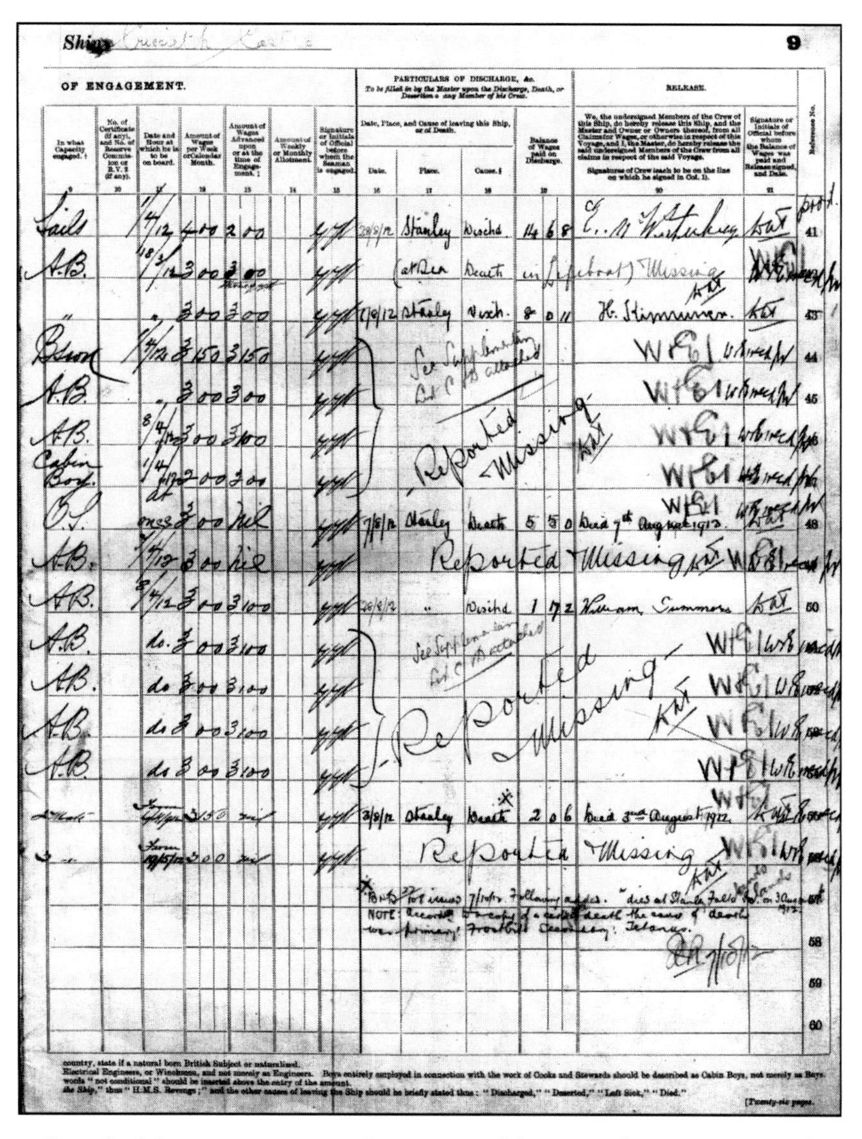

Ship [illegible] 9

OF ENGAGEMENT. | PARTICULARS OF DISCHARGE, &c. *To be filled in by the Master upon the Discharge, Death, or Desertion of any Member of his Crew.* | RELEASE.

In what Capacity engaged. † (9)	No. of Certificate (if any), and No. of Reserve Commission or R.V. 2 (if any). (10)	Date and Hour at which he is to be on board. (11)	Amount of Wages per Week or Calendar Month. (12)	Amount of Wages Advanced upon or at the time of Engagement. ‡ (13)	Amount of Weekly or Monthly Allotment. (14)	Signature or Initials of Official before whom the Seaman is engaged. (15)	Date. (16)	Place. (17)	Cause. § (18)	Balance of Wages paid on Discharge. (19)	We, the undersigned Members of the Crew of this Ship, do hereby release this Ship, and the Master and Owner or Owners thereof, from all Claims for Wages, or otherwise in respect of this Voyage, and I, the Master, do hereby release the said undersigned Members of the Crew from all claims in respect of the said Voyage. Signatures of Crew (each to be on the line on which he signed in Col. 1). (20)	Signature or Initials of Official before whom the Balance of Wages was paid and Release signed, and Date. (21)	Reference No.
Sails		1/4/12	4 0 0	2 0 0		[illegible]	28/8/12	Stanley	Disch'd	14 6 8	[illegible]	KAT	41
A.B.		18/3/12	3 0 0	3 0 0		[illegible]	(at Sea	Death	in Lifeboat) Missing			WFG	42
"		"	3 0 0	3 0 0		[illegible]	1/9/12	Stanley	Disch.	8 0 11	H. [illegible]	KAT	43
Bosun		1/4/12	3 15 0	3 15 0		[illegible]						WFG	44
A.B.		"	3 0 0	3 0 0		[illegible]						WFG	45
A.B.		8/4/12	3 0 0	3 10 0		[illegible]						WFG	46
Cabin Boy		1/4/12	3 0 0	3 0 0		[illegible]						WFG	47
O.S.		at once	3 0 0	nil		[illegible]	7/8/12	Stanley	Death	5 5 0	Died 7th August 1912	KAT	48
A.B.		1/4/12	3 0 0	nil		[illegible]	Reported Missing					WFG	49
A.B.		8/4/12	3 0 0	3 10 0		[illegible]	26/8/12	"	Disch'd	1 7 2	William Summers	KAT	50
A.B.		do.	3 0 0	3 10 0		[illegible]						WFG	51
A.B.		do	3 0 0	3 10 0		[illegible]						WFG	52
A.B.		do	3 0 0	3 10 0		[illegible]						WFG	53
A.B.		do	3 0 0	3 10 0		[illegible]						WFG	54
[illegible]		from [illegible]	3 15 0	nil		[illegible]	3/8/12	Stanley	Death*	2 0 6	Died 3rd August 1912	KAT	55
"		from 19/5/12	3 0 0	nil		[illegible]	Reported Missing					WFG	56
													57
													58
													59
													60

See Supplementary List C (B) attached – Reported Missing (entries 44–47)

See Supplementary List C (B) attached – Reported Missing (entries 51–54)

*[illegible] 7/10/12. Following added: "died at Stanley Falkland Islands on 3 Aug 1912."
NOTE: According to copy of a certificate of death the cause of death was primary frostbite gangrene; Tetanus.

country, state if a natural born British Subject or naturalised.
Electrical Engineers, or Winchmen, and not merely as Engineers. Boys entirely employed in connection with the work of Cooks and Stewards should be described as Cabin Boys, not merely as Boys.
words "not conditional" should be inserted above the entry of the amount.
the Ship," thus "H.M.S. Revenge;" and the other causes of leaving the Ship should be briefly stated thus: "Discharged," "Deserted," "Left Sick," "Died."

[Twenty-six pages.

Page 9 of the crew agreement shows some of the crew who were 'Reported Missing' and the apprentice who died at Stanley, also the crew who were able to sign off in Stanley

Appendix VIII

The *Criccieth Castle* Board of Trade Inquiry 1912

Below is the full text of the Board of Trade Inquiry: The Abandonment Of The Criccieth Castle (No 7561) following the The Merchant Shipping Act, 1894.

In the matter of a Formal Investigation held at Liverpool on the 16th, 17th, 18th, 22nd, 23rd, and 24th October, 1912, before the Stipendiary Magistrate, STUART DEACON, Esquire, assisted by Rear-Admiral FLEET, Captain JOHN TAYLOR, and Captain JOHN HARDY WALKER, into the circumstances attending the abandonment of the British sailing ship *Criccieth Castle* in or about: latitude 54° S, longitude 61° W, South Atlantic Ocean, on or about the 16th July, 1912, whereby loss of life ensued.

Report of Court

The Court having carefully inquired into the circumstances attending the above-mentioned shipping casualty, finds for the reasons stated in the Annex hereto, that the *Criccieth Castle* was abandoned and subsequently, it is presumed, became a total loss in or about latitude 54° 14' S, longitude 61° 24' W, in the South Atlantic Ocean at or about 4 pm on the 16th day of July, 1912. In consequence of such abandonment eight persons lost their lives and seven more are now missing. The immediate cause of the casualty was the breaking of the rudder stock, occasioned by a heavy sea under the port quarter of the vessel striking against the rudder and causing damage as detailed in answer to No 3 of the questions submitted to the Court by the Board of Trade, and the consequent leakage. A Contributing cause to the disaster was, in the opinion of the Court, the fact that the chief mate, although he had received specific instructions from the captain, had omitted to have the bilges in the vicinity of the pump-well properly cleaned in Ballistas of the wheat with which the vessel had been previously laden on her voyage to Callao. The result of such omission was that the water which entered the ship was thereby prevented from getting to or reaching the pump well, and the pumps, when resorted to in order to free this water, were useless. The fact that the wheat had been left in some of the bilges as before mentioned was made known to the captain by the first mate some seven or eight days after the vessel left Ballistas laden with a cargo of guano, and the captain caused efforts to be made on two successive days to have the wheat cleared away, but the men were unable to do the work owing to the unbearable stench caused by the guano or wheat or both of these. The Court feels that the captain might have caused further efforts to be made to clear this wheat away as it is evident to the Court that he was – while not fully cognizant of the extent or nature of the mischief – alive to the possible danger from the wheat to his pumps, although the Court is not prepared to say that the captain, in not making such further efforts was guilty of any actual default. The fact that the pumps, were not earlier resorted to after the happening of the accident is considered by the Court to be in some degree due to the previous knowledge of the captain of the presence of the wheat in the bilges, and it is evident to the Court that such earlier resort, even if it were in fact possible, would have been of no avail. Having said so much, the Court has the satisfaction of further saying that the captain, after the abandonment of the ship had become a necessity, did all in his power to secure the safety of his crew, and the preservation of the lives of those who survive today may be regarded as due to his vigilance and efforts during the terrible ordeal in the lifeboat.

The Court desires to express its sincere sympathy with all those who have lost relatives or friends in this disaster, as well as also with those surviving members of the crew who have endured so much physical suffering.

Dated this 24th day of October, 1912.

STUART DEACON, Judge.

We concur in the above Report.

ERNEST FLEET, Rear-Admiral,)

JOHN TAYLOR,) Assessors

J H WALKER,)

Annex to the Report

This Inquiry was held in the Magistrates Room, and the Municipal Buildings, Dale Street, Liverpool, on the 16th, 17th, 18th, 22nd, 23rd, and 24th days of October, 1912, before Stuart Deacon, Esquire, Stipendiary Magistrate, assisted by Rear-Admiral Fleet, Captain John Taylor, and Captain John H Walker as Nautical Assessors. Mr J Paxton (Avison, Morton, and Paxton) appeared for the Board of Trade; Mr W Cafferata, instructed by Messrs Weightman, Pedder, and Company, represented the owners, Messrs R Thomas and Company; Mr L S Holmes (Miller, Taylor, and Holmes) appeared for the master, Mr Robert Thomas; and Mr W H B Quilliam watched the proceedings on behalf of a number of the survivors of the crew.

The *Criccieth Castle*, Official Number 79127, was a three-masted British sailing ship, built of iron in 1887 by R Williamson and Son, of Workington, Cumberland, her former name being the *Silverdale*. Her length was 263.9 feet, her breadth 39 feet, and her depth in hold from tonnage deck to ceiling at midships 23.7 feet. She was rigged as a ship and registered at the Port of London.

The vessel was assigned a new load line on March 7th, 1907; by Lloyd's Register, the centre of the disc being then placed at 4 feet 10 inches below the statutory deck line, her previous freeboard having been 5 feet $0^1/_2$ inch. She had a forecastle of 26 feet, a deckhouse in which the crew were berthed, and galley adjoining abaft the foremast, and a poop of 47 feet in length. She had one deck and two tiers of beams, and was fitted with a collision bulkhead. She had two main pumps placed immediately abaft the mainmast and was well found as to general equipment. Her tonnage was 1919.77 tons gross and 1877.39 tons register. She had three hatches of the following dimensions: Forehatch, 7 feet 9 inches by 7 feet; main hatch, 16 feet by 11 feet, and afterhatch 8 feet by 7 feet; their respective coamings being two feet high.

She carried three boats – a lifeboat of 26 feet in length, a longboat of 23 feet 3 inches, and a gig, the dimensions of which were not given. The two former were carried on skids under davits between the main and mizzen masts, and the gig was on top of the deckhouse. The lifeboat was fully equipped with oars, mast, sail, &c, in accordance with the Board of Trade requirements, and capable of carrying all the crew. The longboat was equipped in accordance with the regulations, which do not include mast and sail. She was furnished; however, with a mast, and a step for it was fitted in the boat, but she had no sail. It was stated that; the gig had sustained damage during the vessel's previous passage from Port Pirie to Callao, and was not, at the time of the abandonment of the ship, fit for use.

The Ship was supplied with 36 lifebelts, which were kept in the sail locker, six lifebuoys, and the usual complement of rockets and blue-lights; and, according to all the evidence given in Court, was, when she left Ballistas Island, well found in every respect.

She was owned by the Ship Criccieth Castle Company Limited; Mr Robert Thomas, of 26, Chapel Street, Liverpool, being designated the person to whom the management of the vessel was entrusted by and on behalf of the owners under advice received September 1st, 1908, under the seal of the Ship Criccieth Castle Company Limited.

She was classed 100 Al at Lloyd's and passed her second No 2 survey at Antwerp in 1908.

At Leghorn, in March, 1911, she was dry-docked, cleaned, painted, and had her rudder rebushed. This was the last occasion of her being dry-docked.

From Leghorn and Port Empedocle, Sicily, she proceeded to Port Pirie with a cargo of sulphur, and there loaded with wheat for Callao. From Callao she proceeded in ballast to Ballistas Island, Peru, where she took in a cargo of 2,850 tons of guano in bulk for Antwerp. Before commencing to load this cargo, Captain Robert Thomas, who was in charge of the *Criccieth Castle* had occasion to cross over to Pisco to obtain the loading certificate, leaving the vessel in charge of the first mate, to whom, he alleged, he left instructions for the bilges to be thoroughly cleaned out before loading commenced. This order was not fully carried out inasmuch as several bilges in the midship section of the ship were not dealt with at all. The carpenter states that he drew the first mate's attention to the fact that a quantity of wheat, estimated by him as some ten inches in depth still remained in those parts. The first mate is said to have replied that there was no time for it, but that it could be cleared out at sea, and the loading proceeded without any further steps being taken. This fact is confirmed by a statement of the captain's in which he alluded to a conversation with the first mate with reference to the bilges some seven or eight days after leaving Ballistas, when the latter informed the captain of the presence of wheat in the bilges in the vicinity of the pump well.

On June 5th the *Criccieth Castle* left Ballistas for her voyage to Antwerp. Her draught was then 21 feet 8 inches, both forward and aft, and her freeboard was 4 feet $11^1/_2$ inches, her statutory load line being 11 inches above the water line. Her crew then numbered 22 all told, the captain's wife and four-year-old son, who were on board as passengers with the owners' consent, bringing up the total number carried to 24.

Her boats were three in number. The lifeboat, 26 feet long, 7 feet 5 inches broad, and 3 feet deep, had, according to Board of Trade scale, accommodation for 34 adults. She was fully equipped and in good order.

The longboat, 23 feet 3 inches long, 5 feet 9 inches broad, and 2 feet 8 inches in depth, was a boat coming under the heading of a Section D boat. She was also fully equipped according to the Board of Trade requirements but carried no sail although a mast and steps for it had been fitted. The absence of a sail in this boat was considered by the Court to have been a factor of much importance with reference to her subsequent disappearance. This boat had ample accommodation for about 20 persons.

No dimensions are given for the gig, and, indeed, she had been damaged on the previous voyage and had not been repaired.

When seven or eight days out, as before mentioned, the conversation occurred between the captain and first mate in which the latter told the captain that sections of the bilges near the pump well had not been cleaned out and freed from wheat before taking in the cargo of guano. The captain in evidence stated that the first mate had informed him that this had been done on his return from Pisco with the loading certificate. On hearing that the vicinity of the pump well had not been cleared, the captain ordered this work to be undertaken at once, in so far as it was then possible, and William Summers, an AB, was detailed in the first instance for the work. Summers, in his evidence, states that he went down a ventilator on to the fresh water tank immediately abaft the pump well, and from there descended to the bilge and commenced to clear out the wheat. He bailed with a tin into a bucket, which was hauled up the ventilator from above. According to his statement, half was wheat and half water. Coming up at intervals to the top of the water tank to rest and get purer air, he continued down there; a very confined place, for two hours, until his eyes and nose were bleeding from the effects of the foul stench of rotting wheat or of guano or of both, and he was forced to give up the attempt and informed the second mate, who then went down, but he too, owing to the foul smell, came up again at once.

The pumps about this time were tried twice, the captain having found six inches of water to exist on sounding this well, and the carpenter, from his evidence, $4^1/_2$ inches. Very little water came up and it was black and mixed with grain. The captain then ordered a windsail to be put down the ventilator and it remained there all night. Another attempt was made the following day to clear out the wheat, but the foul state of the air still prevented this. No further attempts were made to clear the bilges round the pump well, and the Court is of the opinion that in view of the vital importance of having pumps in proper working order, especially in a vessel with no compartments, more persistent efforts should have been made in this direction, and all doubts as to their being clear or not solved.

According to the evidence of Summers, AB, the pumps had been tried, before leaving port, in the presence of the captain, and would not work, but this is denied by the captain, and not borne out by other evidence.

The weather experienced by the *Criccieth Castle* until reaching the latitude of Valparaiso was, on the whole, fine. From this parallel to Cape Horn, variable and at times boisterous weather was encountered. On July 14th towards midnight the wind according to the captain's evidence; having increased to a heavy gale from the northwest, with a high sea, the upper topsails were furled and at midnight the foresail was clewed up and furled. When in latitude 54° 14' S and longitude 61° 24' W, and at about 0200, according to the captain, but earlier from the account of other witnesses, a heavy sea under the port quarter struck the rudder, breaking the stock immediately under the stern plating, and causing the rudder to bang heavily against the rudder stops, and, as was afterwards ascertained, to open out the shell plates in the vicinity of the sternpost, causing leaking into the after end of the ship, which increased as time wore on. The banging of the rudder continued, it being entirely out of control. Under the impression that the steering gear had become damaged, relieving tackles were hooked on to the tiller when it was then seen that the rudder itself was broken. At the time of the accident the ship was practically hove-to under lower topsails, and fore, main, and mizzen topmast staysails, and making, with leeway, about $1^1/_2$ knots through the water, heading approximately northeast.

Conflicting evidence as to the force of the wind was given, the captain stating that a strong gale was blowing, whilst other witnesses examined described the wind as moderate, but all agreed that a heavy swell was running. As soon as the serious nature of the damage had been ascertained, the crew below were roused out and ordered aft to jettison the cargo, and this work was commenced, using two ventilators abaft the mizzen mast, abreast of each other on the poop and about 18 or 20 inches in diameter.

The captain's idea was to lighten the ship aft as much as possible, but as the amount of cargo he could have expected to get out under these circumstances would be practically infinitesimal, the Court considered these efforts somewhat futile, inasmuch as it would take approximately 18 tons to lighten the vessel an inch.

After working at the cargo four or five hours, the pumps were worked for about an hour, but with no result. The captain stated that when the damage to the rudder occurred the weather was too bad and that there was too much water being shipped to work the pumps in safety, and that it was not until 6.30 am and nearly daylight that orders were given by him to man them. This statement as to the weather being too rough is not borne out by any other witness. They united in fact in agreeing that the pumps could have safely been worked from the time of the breaking of the rudder. The Court's opinion on this subject is fully set forth in the judgement.

At about daylight the carpenter, according to his evidence, went below with the first mate, boatswain and sail maker, and observed about three feet of water in the after hold, though it had not then reached the guano, which did not extend beyond the step of the mizzen mast. At or about 8.46 am, the pumps still being useless, and the water in the ship increasing, the captain, after explaining matters to the crew, decided to take steps to abandon the ship before the darkness of a long mid-winter night set in, and this decision the Court considers, under the circumstances, he was fully justified in coming to.

No steps had been in the meantime taken to secure the rudder. The captain stated that he had considered the matter, but that it was impossible to do anything under the existing circumstances, as the use of a boat under the stern would have been required. He admitted to the Court that had rudder chains been fitted, the damage could have been to a large extent modified.

The Court's remarks as to the value of rudder chains are given in answer to No 3 of the questions submitted by the Board of Trade.

The boats (lifeboat and longboat) having been prepared, provisioned and watered for ten or twelve and with a small quantity of spirits and one bottle of wine, were hoisted out, during which process the lifeboat sustained some damage by striking the davits, causing considerable and constant leakage during her ultimate voyage. The captain considered, in agreement with the first mate, that the crew should be divided, the weather being far too boisterous and uncertain to place the whole of the crew and the two passengers before mentioned in one boat. He therefore ordered the first mate to take charge of the longboat with a crew of six men drawn from his watch, including the third mate, making in all seven persons.

The captain embarked with his wife and son and the remainder of the crew in the lifeboat. During the day a lookout had been placed aloft in the ship to watch for passing vessels, but at no time were signals of distress hoisted or discharged. The boats commenced to leave between 2 pm and 3 pm, and at 4 pm the ship, rolling heavily and deep in water by the stern, was lost sight of. The carpenter stated that before leaving the ship he observed four to five feet of water in the hold aft, and that amidships there was a depth of $2^1/_2$ feet. The afterhatch and poop skylights were opened before leaving. At 5 pm the wind freshened to a fresh gale; the longboat, which had until then been in tow of the lifeboat (both boats pulling), was cast oft with instructions to keep in company. The weather became worse, and at about 6.30 pm the longboat showed a blue light. The lifeboat thereupon closed on her, and on the first mate hailing that he had lost his tiller, another one was thrown to him. At 9 pm the first mate shouted that he was going to heave to as his boat was taking in green seas. The captain replied that the lifeboat was also shipping water, and whilst he was securing a steering oar to its stern, he lost sight of the longboat, which has neither been seen nor heard of since. Both boats were provided with sea anchors and oil for use with them, and in the lifeboat a light was attempted to be shown, but constantly blew out, whilst the blue lights were useless from water. At 9.30 pm the light finally went out and no further attempt could be made to relight it.

At daybreak there was no trace of the longboat the sea was too high for the lifeboat to bear up and look for her.

On this Tuesday morning a grey painted four-masted barque was sighted, homeward bound, and passed at no great distance without observing the boat. Attempts were made by shouting to attract her attention and by hoisting a blanket.

The lifeboat remained hove-to until the Tuesday night, July 16th, when the wind moderated, and at 5 pm a close-reefed sail was set, and the boats headed, as near as the wind would permit, for the Falkland Islands. A chart was in the lifeboat, but the first mate, although he had none in the longboat, was shown the position, of the ship before leaving her, and was told the compass bearing of the Falklands by the captain.

The boat was hove-to again not long after this, and it was not until Thursday that the journey could be resumed. It would be as well here to allude to the deaths occurring from extreme cold, wet, and exposure during and after this passage. J Answorth was the first to succumb on Tuesday night the 16th July. He had been ill before leaving the ship. Some little time before he died, and in his delirium and semi-conscious state, he rolled overboard, but was hauled in again and placed along the side of the boat, but he succumbed about 7 pm. His death was followed quickly by that of P J Subra, the cook and steward, and of Nakarate, the Japanese cabin boy, both, from their calling, unused to exposure. They were buried about four hours afterwards, their bodies being gently dropped over the side. There were no stimulants left at this time, the small quantity taken having been issued on the first night out, a half-bottle of port only reserved for the captain's wife and boy in case of extreme emergency. On Wednesday E Kannegiesser, AB, died, and was buried five or six hours afterwards. Joseph Smith, AB, was the next to succumb at 11 pm on Wednesday. He was buried at daylight on Thursday. J Roberts, AB, died at 2 am on October 22nd, and was buried six hours afterwards, when six miles from land. F G Lord, second mate, and Juan Cecchi, OS, died in hospital at Port Stanley, Falkland Islands, on August 3rd and 7th respectively, both from the effects of cold and exposure experienced in the boat. This brought the total number of deaths amongst the crew of the lifeboat to eight.

Resuming the account of the lifeboat's voyage, sail was again made on Thursday, the boat having been hove-to most of the time since leaving with sea anchor and the occasional use of oil. On Saturday the 20th July, at daylight, Beauchêne Island, 240 feet high and 30 miles south of the Falklands, was sighted. On Saturday afternoon the 20th July the boat landed at an uninhabited spot on East Falklands, about 25 miles south of Cape Pembroke Lighthouse. Here the crew remained all night amongst the snow. The captain and carpenter went inland at 8 am on the 21st to reconnoitre, but returned at noon. At 2 pm a vessel was observed in the offing, and the boat put off toward her, but failed to attract attention. An attempt was then made to reach the shore again but the wind had freshened from off the land. On Monday morning the captain, estimating that they would have been driven 60 miles off the land, was surprised to sight it only five miles away, the wind having changed during the night. The boat finally landed near Pembroke Lighthouse, Port Stanley, after a week of terrible suffering to her crew.

Expert evidence was given during the trial as to the effect of guano mixed with salt water from leakage, and of the manner in which that might affect the working of the pumps, it having been the captain's contention that the non-working of the pumps was due almost entirely to this cause, but the Court were unanimously of opinion that it was the grain in the bilge that prevented their proper working.

No lifebelts were taken in the boats when the ship was abandoned, the captain stating that he did not consider them necessary.

One witness, Summers, AB, stated that he asked the captain for one, but this the captain denied. One lifebuoy was said to have been in each boat.

During the perilous voyage in the lifeboat many of the crew including the captain, through strain and exposure, suffered from extraordinary delusions. The captain on one occasion was washed or fell out of the boat, but was hauled in again. His little boy of four probably owed his survival to being wrapped up in the dead men's oilskins.

The following is a detailed list of the crew who lost their lives in the lifeboat and longboat, and who died in hospital at Port Stanley, Falkland Islands.

Name	Age	Rating	Nationality
	Died in lifeboat		
J Arnfors	21	AB	Finland
P J Subra	52	Cook & Steward	London
Nakarate	25	Cabin boy	Japan
E Kannegiesser	20	AB	Stettin
J Roberts	38	AB	Anglesea
Joseph Smith	49	AB	Liverpool
	Died at Port Stanley		
Frederick Sainsbury Lord	20	2nd Mate	Sunderland
Juan Cecchi	19	OS	Ancona
	Missing with longboat		
William A Gale	26	1st Mate	Isle of Man
Fred U Hellyer	20	3rd Mate	Hull
J W Wilson	43	Boatswain	Jersey

C Borjerson	23	AB	Sweden
George Powell	32	AB	Cardiff
S Martin	39	AB	London
T Barker	53	AB	Rhode Is

At the conclusion of the evidence, Mr Paxton, for the Board of Trade, submitted the following questions for the opinion of the Court.

1. What was the Cost of the vessel to her owners? What was her value when she sailed on her last voyage? What insurances were effected upon and in connection with her?

2. When the vessel left Ballistas Islands on or about 5th June last -

(a) Was she in good and seaworthy condition as regards hull and equipments?

(b) Had she the required freeboard, and was she in good trim for a voyage to Antwerp?

(c) Were the bilges properly cleaned out, the pump well properly protected, and the pumps in good working order?

(d) Were the boats in good condition, properly equipped, and sufficient for the number of persons on board?

(e) Was the ship properly provided with lifebelts and buoys?

3. What was the cause of the rudder post breaking on the 16th July last? What damage was thereby caused to the hull? Might such damage have been avoided if the rudder had been fitted with rudder chains? Did the master under the circumstances make every reasonable effort to get the rudder under control and to repair same?

4. What was the cause of the pumps getting choked, and was it possible, under the circumstances, for the master to do anything effective to clear them?

5. When and where was the vessel abandoned? What was her general condition at that time? Was she prematurely abandoned?

6. Should lifebelts and/or lifebuoys have been taken in the boats?

7. Was the vessel navigated with proper and seamanlike care?

8. What were the circumstances in which (1) eight members of the crew lost their lives, and (7) seven others are missing?

9. Was the abandonment of the sailing ship *Criccieth Castle* and/or the loss of life caused by the wrongful act or default of the master?

Mr W Cafferata and Mr L S Holmes having addressed the Court on behalf of the owners and master respectively, the Court gave judgement as above, and returned the following answers, to the questions of the Board of Trade.

1. The cost of the vessel was £18,500 in 1889, when the vessel was taken over by her present owners. No evidence as to the actual value of the vessel when she sailed on her last voyage was before the Court, but she was valued for insurance purposes at £9,400.

The insurance effected upon her was as follows: In case of total loss the sum of £4,700 was insured with Mutual Insurance Clubs. A further one-fourth of her value, namely £2,350, was divided between ten single ship companies (including the Ship Criccieth Castle Company), over which the vessel's owners are the managers.

The freight from Ballistas was valued at £3,325, of which £1,500 alone was insured, and this in the Mutual Insurance Clubs referred to. There was no insurance on disbursements.

2. From the evidence produced in Court:

(a) The vessel was in good and seaworthy condition as regards the hull and equipments?

(b) She had the required freeboard, and was in good trim for a voyage.

(c) The evidence on these points is conflicting, but the Court's conclusions are as follows: The bilges, after the vessel had discharged a cargo of grain in Callao, were properly cleared with the exception of some amidships in the vicinity of the pump and pump well in which the wheat, which had formed part of the previous cargo with which the ship had been laden, had been left to a depth apparently of ten inches or more, with the result that any water collecting in the ship was thereby prevented from reaching the pump well; although the pumps themselves were apparently in good working order. There is nothing in the evidence to show that pump well itself was otherwise than properly protected.

(d) The lifeboat and longboat were in good condition, but the gig was not, for it was damaged on the passage to Callao, and was not repaired. The boats were properly equipped and more than sufficient for the persons on board so far as compliance with any of the regulations of the Board of Trade. The Court, however, thinks it right; here to add that the evidence shows that the longboat, although it was provided with a mast, was not provided with a sail, and further that if such boat had in fact been provided with a sail there was, in the opinion of many of the witnesses, a probability, or at any rate a possibility, that the boat would have safely, reached the Falkland Islands, and the lives of those on board have thus been saved. Having regard to the fact, which much impressed the Court, that the lifeboat under the circumstances proved to be an unsafe refuge for the whole of the persons on board the vessel, the absence of a sail for the longboat became a factor of great importance.

(e) The ship was provided with 86 lifebelts and six lifebuoys.

3. The cause of the stock of the rudder breaking on the 15th July was a heavy sea under the port quarter of the vessel striking the rudder. The damage thereby caused was the breaking of the rudder stock at a point immediately below the counter, which caused the rudder to be out of control and to strike heavily against the rudder stops on either side, thus opening out the shell plates of the vessel in the vicinity of the sternpost, and letting in water at a constantly increasing ratio. The Court thinks that much of such damage might have been avoided if the rudder had been fitted with rudder chains, and this was also the opinion expressed by the

master, but as far as the Court has been able to ascertain, rudder chains are now regarded as obsolete, and are seldom fitted. According to the statement of the master he made no effort to get the rudder under control and repair the same, because no such effort, in his opinion, would, under the circumstances of the case, have been of any avail.

4. The evidence on these points was most conflicting, but the Court has come to the conclusion that the pumps were not in fact choked at all, but that the wheat which had been left in some of the sections of the bilges, as described in answer to question 2 was in such quantity as to prevent any water there might be in the vessel getting to or reaching the pump well, so as to be sucked up by the pumps. The master learnt from the first officer for the first time, when the vessel had been out from Ballistas for about, seven or eight days; that the bilges had not been properly cleared of the wheat in question, and he caused more than one effort to be made to get the wheat cleared out, but owing to the stench caused either by the guano alone, or by the guano and the rotting wheat combined, the men sent down to clear out the wheat were unable to remain below for a sufficient length of time to do the work required and the effort was consequently abandoned. The Court while it believes that the master was unaware of the exact state of circumstances which were affecting his pumps, is satisfied that he was none the less alive to the unsatisfactory state of affairs existing by reason of the wheat having been left in the bilges, and this being so, he might, in the opinion of the Court, have persevered further with his efforts to clear the wheat away. The Court however is not prepared to say that the master, in not making farther effort, was guilty of any actual default.

5. The vessel was abandoned in the South Atlantic Ocean at about 4 pm of the 15th July, 1912, in or about latitude 54° 14' S and longitude 61° 24' W. She was at that time taking in water at an increasingly rapid rate, and was uncontrollable; she was not, having regard to the circumstances, prematurely abandoned.

6. A life buoy was placed in each of the boats. Lifebelts were not taken because the captain thought that they would be of no use, but the Court is of opinion that they should have been taken and each person supplied with one.

7. There is nothing to show that the vessel was not navigated with proper and seamanlike care.

8. (1) The circumstances under which eight members of the crew lost their lives were that, in the abandonment, 17 persons, who included the captain, his wife and child, who were on board, and who survived, took refuge in the lifeboat, and were exposed to the rigours of midwinter and bad weather until they landed at Port Stanley at or about 4 pm on the 22nd July, 1912. Six of such 17 persons died during the time of such exposure, and two subsequently died from the effects of such exposure after being placed in hospital at Port Stanley. (2) The remaining seven persons took refuge in the longboat owing to the fact that it was not considered safe for all to go in the lifeboat, and it is surmised that they lost their lives some time after 9 pm on the night of the 15th July owing to the boat being submerged or capsized, inasmuch as although they were in the company of the lifeboat more or less until the time last mentioned neither they nor the boat have ever since been heard of.

9. The abandonment of the sailing ship *Criccieth Castle* and the loss of life which thereby ensued, was not, in the opinion of the Court, caused by any wrongful act or default of the master.

STUART DEACON, Judge.

We concur in the above Report.

ERNEST FLEET, Rear-Admiral,)

JOHN TAYLOR,) Assessors

J H WALKER,)

(Issued in London by the Board of Trade on the 22nd day of November, 1912.)

Appendix IX

Notes On Recent Wreck Inquiries

From *The Mercantile Marine Service Association Reporter*, Volume 38 1913, pp 38-43

The *Criccieth Castle* was an iron-built three-masted sailing vessel, ship rigged, of London; 1,920 tons gross and 1,877 tons nett register; launched in 1877 at Workington; managed by Messrs R Thomas and Company for a Single-ship Limited Company. On March 7th, 1907, she was assigned a new load-line by Lloyd's Register, giving her a freeboard of 4 feet 10 inches, her previous freeboard having been 5 feet $0^1/_2$ inch. She had a raised forecastle 26 feet long, a deck-house for crew, and galley, and a poop of 47 feet in length, one deck, two tiers of beams and a collision bulkhead, two main pumps just abaft the mainmast, three hatchways with coaming 2 feet above deck, one lifeboat 26 feet, one longboat 23 feet 3 inches, and one gig. The two large boats were carried on skids, under davits, between the main and mizzen masts, and the gig was stowed on the top of the deck-house. The lifeboat had mast and sail, and was capable of carrying all the crew, but the longboat had a mast but no sail, as the Board of Trade regulations do not require it. The gig was damaged, and at the time of the abandonment was unfit for service. Thirty-six lifebelts and six lifebuoys, with the regular complement of rockets and blue lights, formed the rest of the life-saving outfit, and when she left Ballistas Island with a cargo of guano and a crew of 22 hands (all told), bound to Antwerp, the ship was in good seaworthy condition and well found. She had passed her second (No 2) survey at Antwerp in 1908, and was classed 100 A1 at Lloyds.

In March, 1911, she was dry docked, cleaned, painted, and rudder rebushed at Leghorn, and loaded a cargo of sulphur for Port Pirie, and on arrival at the latter port loaded wheat for Callao. From Callao she sailed in ballast to Ballistas Island, Peru, and there loaded guano in bulk (2,850 tons) for Antwerp.

The master had occasion, to go to Pisco to get his loading certificate, and before leaving he charged the mate to clear all out of the limbers and bilges before commencing to load guano. This order was not fully carried out, large sections of the bilges remaining untouched, and this remissness or neglect was not known to the master until after the ship had sailed from Ballistas, when the mate reported the presence of wheat in the bilges in the vicinity of the pump well – contrary to a previous report to the master.

On June 5th they left Ballistas, drawing 2l feet 3 inches fore and aft with a freeboard of 4 feet 11½ inches, the legal load-line being 1½ inches free of the water level. She carried the master's wife and child as passengers, besides the crew of 22 hands; the lifeboat (26 feet by 7 feet 5 inches by 3 feet) could accommodate 34 persons, and longboat 20 persons.

On receiving the mate's report that the wheat had not been cleared out of the vicinity of the pumps, an attempt was made to bail some of it out, but the overpowering stench of rotting wheat and guano drove the men on deck. The pumps threw very little water – black coloured and mixed with grain; the sounding rod showed six inches. An attempt was then made to ventilate the pumpwell by means of a windsail, and another effort to clean the bilges, but failed through the foulness of the air below.

They experienced fine weather until past the latitude of Valparaiso, and then rough and changeable weather was encountered up to Cape Horn. Around midnight on July 14th a heavy gale from the northwest with high sea, ship under lower topsails, furled the foresail, and when in latitude 54° 14' S, and longitude 61° 24' W, at 2 am, the rudder stock was broken just under the stern plating by shock of heavy sea striking the rudder, which then banged heavily against the rudder stops and opened out the plating in the vicinity, causing leakage, which gradually increased. The ship was then fore reaching under lower topsails and storm staysails, making $1^{1}/_{2}$ knots (most of which was leeway), and heading about northeast.

The crew were turned up, and set to jettison cargo, using the two after ventilators (about 18 or 20 inches in diameter) for the work. Naturally the amount of cargo handled was small indeed, the idea being to lighten the ship aft. After five hours of this work they tried the pumps for about an hour without freeing the ship, and at daylight they found 3 feet water in after hold, but not yet up to the guano. At 8.45, pumps useless and leakage increasing, the master decided to abandon the vessel while he had daylight, and before the long winter night set in, and the Court held that he was fully justified by the circumstances. The master stated that he could do nothing to stop the leakage as the service of a boat under the stern was needed, and this was impossible, had rudder chains been filled the control of the rudder might have been attained.

They cleared away the two large boats and provisioned them for ten or twelve days, a small amount of spirits and a bottle of wine, and in hoisting them out the lifeboat sustained damage by striking the davits, which caused considerable and constant leakage.

The master and mate agreed to divide the crew rather than risk all lives in one boat in bad weather. The mate took charge of the longboat, with a crew of six men, including the third mate making a total of seven persons. The master took the rest of the crew, his wife and little four-year-old son with him in the lifeboat.

No vessels were in sight from aloft, and the boats left the ship between 2 and 3 pm on the 15th July, 1912, and at 4 pm they lost sight of the ship, which when last seen was rolling heavily and down by the stern, with 5 feet water aft, but only $2^{1}/_{2}$ feet amidships when last examined by the carpenter. The afterhatch and the poop skylights were left open when abandoning the ship.

At 5 pm the wind freshened to a gale, and the longboat (hitherto attached to the lifeboat) was cast off, but directed to keep close. At 6.30 pm the longboat showed a blue light, had lost his tiller, was supplied with another, and at 9 pm the mate shouted that he must heave-to, as his boat was shipping heavy water.

Presently they lost sight of the longboat, which was never seen again. Both boats had sea anchors and oil on board, and the blue lights in the lifeboat were useless from water; they tried to keep other lights burning, but they were blown out.

At daylight the sea was too heavy to allow searching for the longboat, and during the morning a four-masted barque passed at no great distance without observing them, although they shouted and hoisted a blanket to draw her attention.

She remained hove-to till 5 pm on July 16th, when weather allowed them to proceed under close-reefed sail towards the Falkland Islands. They had a chart, and had instructed the mate (who had none in the longboat) how to steer by compass to make the Falklands. Thus they proceeded, suffering intensely from extreme cold, wet and exposure, having to heave to when sea and wind were too heavy. On July 16th J Arnfor, AB, aged 21, died in delirium, and soon the cook and steward, Subra, age 52, and the Japanese cabin boy, age 25, and their bodies were passed overboard. Three more able seamen then succumbed to their privations, and were buried in the sea.

The second mate, F G Lord, age 20, and Juan Cecchi, OS (Austrian), died in hospital at Port Stanley from the effects of cold and exposure. Thus eight men perished out of the total of 15 persons in the lifeboat. On the 20th July Beauchêne Island, 30 miles south of the Falklands, was sighted at daylight, and during the afternoon of the same day they landed on an uninhabited part of the East Falklands, about 25 miles south of Cape Pembroke Lighthouse and remained all night in the snow, and on the 21st, failing to find human assistance, they put out at 2 pm to try to get to a vessel in the offing; they failed in this, and their return to shore was cut off by the wind freshening from the land, but the next day found themselves only five miles from shore, as the wind had shifted during the night. Finally they managed to land near Pembroke Lighthouse, Port Stanley, in a pitiable state, after a week of terrible experiences and suffering.

The Court held that it was the grain alone that choked the pumps and not the guano. No lifebelts were taken in the boats when the ship was abandoned. One lifebuoy was assigned to each boat. The child passenger was wrapped up in the oilskins of the men who died. The small quantity of stimulants was issued to the crew on the first night out, only half a bottle of port being reserved for the captain's wife and child.

After hearing Counsel for the parties concerned, the Court gave judgement. The *Criccieth Castle* in 1889 cost £18,500, when purchased by her present owners, and the value for insurance when she sailed on her last voyage was £9,400. She was insured in Mutual Clubs for £4,700, in case of total loss, and for £2,350, divided among ten Single Ship Companies managed by the Owners (including the Ship Criccieth Castle Company). Freight from Ballistas, £3,325; of which £1,500 only was insured in Mutual Clubs. Disbursements not covered. (1) The vessel left port in good and seaworthy condition of hull and equipments. She had the requisite freeboard and was in good trim for the voyage, but portions of the bilges in the vicinity of the pumps were choked with wheat, to the extent of some ten inches or more, so that the water was prevented from reaching the pumpwell, although the pumps were in good working order and the pumpwell was properly protected. The lifeboat and longboat were in good condition, but the gig was damaged and unserviceable. The larger boats were properly equipped and more than sufficient for all persons on board, but, although complying with the Regulations the Court expressed a strong opinion that the longboat ought to have been provided with a sail, the want of which probably accounted for the boat failing to reach the Falklands. The lifebelts and lifebuoys were sufficient. (2) For cause of rudder stock breaking and leakage see foregoing narrative. The Court remarked that rudder chains are now obsolete and are seldom fitted. (3) After examining much conflicting evidence the Court concluded that the pumps were not choked at all, but that the wheat in the bilges prevented the water reaching them. The Court believes that the master was not aware that his orders to clear the bilges, before loading guano, had not been complied with, but opined that he might have shown more perseverance in his efforts to clear them at sea, but did not regard this as actual default. (4) Ship abandoned in South Atlantic at 4 pm on July 15th, 1912, in latitude 54° 14' S, longitude 61° 24' W, uncontrollable and making water rapidly. She was not prematurely abandoned; lifebelts should have been supplied to all persons in the boats. The ship was not navigated in a careless or improper manner. (5) The details of the experiences in the boats have been given (with the loss of life) in the narrative of the disaster. The Court found that the abandonment of the *Criccieth Castle* and ensuing loss of life were not caused by default of the master.

Appendix X

British Roll of Honour

Lieutenant Robert Thomas of the Royal Naval Reserve

Lieutenant Robert Thomas, who was killed in action in the North Sea after a life of stirring adventure, was the son of the late Captain Robert Thomas and of Mrs Roberts, of Lonsdale, Criccieth, where he was born on May 6th 1879 and where he also received his education.

Belonging to a seafaring family, his father and grandfather having been Master Mariners before him, Lieutenant Thomas commenced his own nautical career at the early age of 13, when he served on the Portmadoc Schooner for four years, during which period he experienced several exciting adventures.

Subsequently he joined the firm of Messrs Robert Thomas and Company, of Liverpool, and after serving in the *Criccieth Castle*, *Denbigh Castle* and the *Eduryfed*, was given command of the *Eifion* at the age of twenty-four, his first voyage with his ship being a memorable one. He left Garston for Valparaiso on June 14th, 1904, and after encountering a terrible storm off Cape Horn, which swept away all the boats, it was discovered that the vessel was on fire, and for three days the crew were obliged to remain on board, battling with the flames and in great peril. Eventually a Liverpool ship, the *Lonsdale*, was sighted, and after considerable difficulty the crew of the *Eifion* were rescued, the incident being considered the bravest deed of the year. At the Naval Court of Inquiry, held in October at Valparaiso, it was found that Lieutenant Thomas had navigated his ship in a seamanlike and proper manner, doing everything in his power to save the ship and the lives of the crew.

Lieutenant Thomas was then placed in command of the *Criccieth Castle*, of which vessel he remained master for a period of nine years. On March 26th, 1907, he married Katherine, daughter of Mr and Mrs W J Pritchard, of Llangybi, Chwilog, Carnarvonshire, who accompanied him nearly all over the world, and with their little son was present on the last voyage of the *Criccieth Castle*. On this occasion the vessel was on a voyage from Ballestas Islands to Falmouth, and was manned by a crew of twenty-eight men all told. On July 15th, 1912, she encountered very heavy gales off Cape Horn, and as the result of the extensive damage sustained had to be abandoned in a derelict condition. Lieutenant Thomas took with him in one boat his wife and child and 14 members of the crew. The other boats became separated and were lost, but Lieutenant Thomas' after remaining afloat for over a week, during which period the occupants suffered severely from exposure, privations and other perils, reached Stanley, Falkland Islands, whence they were able to return home. An interesting and detailed account of their fight with death was written by Lieutenant Thomas and published in The Wide World Magazine.

The strain and exposure, however, told on his health, and for some months he was incapacitated from service, then he joined an Oil Tanker, but was not yet in a fit condition to stand the rigours of another voyage, and his health again broke down, compelling him to rest for 18 months. By that time the world was engulfed in War, and he took a Commission as Lieutenant in the Royal Naval Reserve, and was made Commanding Officer of *HMS Kelvin*. In this capacity he rendered very able service, and on one occasion was instrumental in salving a portion of a seaplane whose engines were out of order. He also rendered aid to several brother sailors who were in danger of drowning through the sinking of their vessel by a German mine, and was the recipient of many grateful letters of appreciation.

On July 3rd, 1917, he was hurt by a mine explosion, but he remained on duty, and four days later, on July 7th, made the supreme sacrifice willingly and cheerfully for King and Country.

His death was widely mourned, for he had won friends in all parts of the world by his happy, cheerful and genial disposition. The Commander-in-Charge at Harwich wrote to Mrs. Thomas:

'It would be impossible for me to speak too highly of the very real and manly service of your late husband during his long and dangerous service at Harwich.'

From their Majesties the King and Queen came a gracious message of sympathy, whilst my Lords Commissioners of the Admiralty wrote:

'That Lieutenant Thomas has shown great zeal and courage in the performance of his dangerous duties.'

From the Commander of Auxiliary Patrols at Harwich came the following:

'He was a most gallant officer beloved by everybody, untiring in zeal and devotion to duty, and of the many officers I have had here none carried out orders more explicitly and faithfully than he did. His loss is a very grievous one to the nation besides yourself... Had he lived he would have undoubtedly received the Distinguished Service Order, which he had earned by his gallantry at all times.'

In warm appreciation, a brother officer writes of Lieutenant Thomas as:

'A grand fellow... always so keen and willing and capable at this terrible work of mine sweeping.'

Lieutenant Thomas' body was recovered, and he was taken home and laid to rest at Capel Helyg Cemetery, Llangybi, Chwilog, with impressive ceremonial, a naval party from his own ship being present. Mr William George, brother of the prime Minister, in addressing the naval escort, paid warm tribute to the noble character and happy disposition of Lieutenant Thomas.

'Great heart that sprang to Duty's call;

With thought of all the best in him

That time shall have no power to dim;

With thought of duty nobly done,

And high Eternal Welfare won.'

The memorial to Robert Thomas in Capel Helyg cemetery, Llangybi

Appendix XI

Funeral Notice of Captain Thomas

This is taken from a newspaper cutting that was found in the Pritchard family Bible.

The remains of the late Captain Robert Thomas (Lieutenant, RNR), who was killed whilst on duty in the North Sea on the 7th inst, were interred at Llangybi, near Criccieth, on Monday.

The Rev Thomas Williams officiated, assisted by the Revs John Davies (rector), R G Roberts, Carnarvon; John Owen, Carnarvon; Morgan-Price, and other ministers.

The chief mourner were Mrs Thomas and Mrs Thomas' mother, brothers and sisters. The Navy was represented at the funeral by Lieutenant Griffiths of Criccieth and four Naval Reserve men from Lieutenant Thomas' ship.

Amongst the other mourners present were Mr Owain Hughes and W Mallet, Portmadoc; John Evans, Capt Jones, Borth, Capt Jones, ditto; Mr Morris, Portmadoc representing the Masonic Brotherhood; Mr William George, Dr Livingstone Davies, Mr Burnell, Mr Goodwill, Capt T J Evans, Capt Jack Roberts, Mr W H Williams, Manchester House; Mr W H Williams, Wellington Terrace; Capt Davies, Mr D P Williams, Mr Hugh Jones, Mr Owen Roberts, Festiniog; Mr Owen Jones, Pwllheli; Mr William Jones, do.; Capt Jones, Talafor; Capt Griffiths, Brynafon; Dr Rowlands, Plas Llanaelhaiarn; Mr Pierce, Pencaenewydd; Mr Willians, Capel Helyg Farm; Mr William, Tynyporth; Mr Williams, Cefn Coch; Mr J Parry, Pencaenewydd; Mr R Parry, ditto; Mr R Jones, Glanygors; Mr John Evans, Gwyrnallt; Mr John Jones, Bodoven; Mr Owen Hughes, Llangybi; Mr John Jones, Tu-hwnt-I'r-Mynydd; Mr Robt Jones, Llanarmon; Mr D J Jones, Brynllefrith; Rev D R Griffith, Penmaenmawr; Mr R J George, Carnarvon; Mr R W Davies, Pant; Mr Owen Barton, Mr William Williams, Capt Williams, Bryn Beune, Carnarvon.

Wreaths were sent by the following: Widow and children; all at

Lonsdale; and Bryn Gwalia; Admiral Cayley, officers and men of the Harwich Patrol vessels and minesweepers; Lieutenant Griffiths; Freemasons; Mr Owen Jones, Pwllheli, and others etc.

A striking tribute was paid to the deceased by the Masonic Brotherhood, and Mr William George, addressing the naval escort, referred to the noble character and happy disposition of the late Captain Thomas.

Mrs Thomas (widow) has received the following letter of sympathy from the Commander-in-Chief, Harwich:

'Dear Mrs Thomas, It is with feeling of great personal loss that I write to tender my very deep sympathy with you in your deep bereavement. It would be impossible for me to speak too highly of the manly service of your late husband during his long and dangerous service at Harwich. There are many here who will mourn the loss of a very gallant officer and comrade. Believe me, with renewed expression of deep sympathy, Yours sincerely, CUTHBERT CAYLEY (Rear Admiral)'

Deep sympathy is felt for the widow and three little ones in their bereavement.

The late Captain Thomas was master of the *Criccieth Castle*, which was lost on July 15, 1912, about 300 miles to the east of Staten Island. The vessel was on a voyage from Ballestas Islands for Falmouth for orders, and was manned by a crew of 28 men all told. The captain was accompanied by his wife and child. The ship encountered very heavy gales off Cape Horn, and as the result of the extensive damage sustained she had to be abandoned in a derelict condition. Capt Thomas took with him in one boat his wife and child and 14 members of the crew. The other boat became separated, and after being adrift for over a week, during which time the occupants suffered severely from exposure and privations, the master's boat reached Stanley, Falkland Islands.

Robert's body was buried in Llangybi Chapel cemetery, and the memorial has this inscription: *'In loving and affectionate memory of Lieutenant Robert Thomas RNR commanding Officer of HMS*

Kelvin. The dearly beloved and devoted husband of Catherine Thomas 'Gorsannedd' Llangybi died on the 7th day of July 1917, nobly and bravely made the supreme sacrifice in his country's cause whilst on active service in the North Sea aged 38 years. Priod a thad mâd ym medd, un anwyl â gwenau tangnefedd; wcus siom! Gwâg yw ei sedd sy' heno yn Gorsannedd, Isfryn (translation - A good husband and father is in his grave, a fond one with peaceful smiles, such a misfortune! Empty tonight is his seat that's in Gorsannedd. By Isfryn) He, being made perfect in a short time, fulfilled a long time.'

Capel Helyg, Llangybi, where Catherine and Robert first met and where they and their offspring are buried

Appendix XII

An Interesting Relic

(from The Falkland Islands Magazine and Church Paper, April 1915)

We publish below a letter addressed by H E the Governor to the Hon Secretary of the Museum Committee. It will be within the recollection of all our readers how and in what circumstances the boat in question arrived here. This gift will be a reminder of a sad and heroic struggle of people, many of whom perished in the attempt to reach our shores:

Government House, Stanley, 26th February 1915

Sir, As you will recollect, the barque Criccieth Castle foundered in heavy weather on the Burwood Bank, which is south-southwest of the Falklands, on the 15th July 1912. Captain Thomas, his wife and child, the second Officer, the carpenter, and 12 seamen (17 in all) embarked in the ship's lifeboat, while the First Officer, and six of the crew got into another boat which was lost. The Criccieth Castle was abandoned in a sinking condition on the Monday afternoon, and on the following Monday, after eight days of terrible exposure and suffering during which five men died, and Captain Thomas was washed overboard but fortunately was recovered, the lifeboat with all its survivors very badly frost-bitten, managed to reach Cape Pembroke and entered the gulch there, where they were aided and assisted by the Lighthouse keepers. Of those who reached the land two subsequently succumbed while in Hospital. The boat was afterwards badly damaged on the rocks in the gulch, and on being brought to Stanley was put up to auction and purchased by the Government.

I had intended to have her repaired and put in good order, as she was well built and of teak, and made available as a lifeboat for Stanley, having in view her seaworthiness and the absence of anything of the sort locally. During my absence from the Colony however she was condemned, and on my return from leave in

April 1914, I found her lying outside, and very much the worse for exposure to the weather, and learnt that she was destined to be broken up for firewood. As I considered that it was a mistake to destroy a boat with so unique a record I took possession of her and have had her repaired and painted at my own expense as I desire to present her to the Falkland Museum on behalf of the Colonists.

Should your Committee be willing to accept the gift, kindly let me know where you would like the boat placed, and after putting her there, I will formally hand her over to your Committee. I attach a copy of The Falkland Islands Magazine for August 1912, which contains an account of the loss of the Criccieth Castle.

I am, Sir,

Yours very truly,

W L Allardyce

The lifeboat at Stanley

There is a photograph of the lifeboat taken in about 1920 standing at the back of the old Stanley Town Hall. Apparently the lifeboat was on display on Ross Road, Stanley, for many years and was broken up for firewood at some date around 1951. Prior to this there is a story that the boat was sawn in half for an amateur dramatic presentation.

The lifeboat at the back of the old Stanley Town Hall in about 1920 (Jim Elliott Collection)

In about 1950 two young men 'liberated' the ship's badge from the front of the boat. Then a few years ago they must have realised what they had done as the badge was sent to the museum where it can be seen to this day. The badge is a copy of the Robert Thomas 'house' or company flag which was flown from the peak of the main mast. It is a fine example of how the crew with encouragement from the captain would titivate the ship.

The 'liberated' badge from the front of the lifeboat (from the Falkland Islands Museum & National Trust Cobb Collection).

The Robert Thomas and Company 'house' or company flag which was flown from the top of the main mast of all their ships and copied on the lifeboat's badge. The flag was red and yellow with dark blue around the anchor

Appendix XIII

Cape Pembroke Lighthouse

The first lighthouse on Cape Pembroke was built in 1855 after the nearby Billy Rock offshore had claimed 15 ships. The original light used rape seed oil, but as it burnt a thousand gallons a year, sea lion oil was attempted as a substitute.

The original Cape Pembroke lighthouse before it was rebuilt in 1906

In 1904 the wooden piles comprising the foundations of the lighthouse were found to be rotten owing to the damp weather and the lighthouse was rebuilt in 1906. It was a major undertaking, involving some 700 tons of new materials, a Trinity House supervisor and four contractors from Britain, and a team of local men. A lightship light was placed on the peninsula while work was in progress.

An old postcard showing Cape Pembroke Lighthouse from the Gulch in fine weather!

The re-erected tower was positioned about 200 yards to the west of the original site and a new lantern was placed on top, making the lighthouse 70 feet high from base to weather vane. The rebuilt light was finally illuminated again in June 1907. The original system had been replaced by a dioptric (refracting) third order apparatus, lit by paraffin lamps. Mounted on a stand which revolved by clockwork, it showed a flashing light instead of a fixed one and was visible for 16 miles in clear weather. The tower was painted black with a broad white band. In this form it operated continuously until the Argentine invasion in April 1982, when it was put out of operation. A small lighthouse keeper's cottage stood beside it.

The Cape Pembroke Lighthouse in 1987. The water-filled rut was the 'main road' from Stanley to the lighthouse (Jim Elliott Collection)

A Trinity House Survey in 1983 proposed the installation of a new light in the tower, but before any action could be taken the lighthouse was badly vandalised and most of the prism and lantern glass were smashed leaving the tower open to the elements. In 1990 a programme of restoration was begun, financed partly by charities and partly by the Falkland Islands Government's Historic Buildings Fund. The original aim was to restore the light as a navigational aid, but after much deliberation and consultation with Trinity House it was decided that it would not be practical.

Today the light at Cape Pembroke is a free standing solar powered unit erected by the Fisheries Department in 1987. It was decided that the lighthouse had become redundant as a navigational aid and the new unit instead of a light has a racon. A racon is a radar transponder commonly used to mark maritime navigational hazards. The word is comes from RAdar and beaCON.

The racon at Cape Pembroke today (Jim Elliott Collection)

Appendix XIV

The Loss of the *Kate Thomas*

The following is an article entitled 'Shipping Disaster off Land's End - Many Lives Lost' that appeared in The Times newspaper on 5th April 1910:

There was landed at Falmouth yesterday by the Belgian tug *John Bull* the only survivor of a shipping disaster which occurred off the Longships early yesterday morning. The four-masted barque *Kate Thomas*, owned by Kate Thomas Sailing Ship Company (Messrs W Thomas Sons and Company Limited) of Liverpool, was being towed from Antwerp to Port Talbot in ballast, when she was run into by a steamer, and she sank in about a quarter of an hour. A young apprentice named Jack Nelson, of Birkenhead, was the only survivor. He swam to the tug and was rescued, but the remainder of the crew, numbering 18 or 19 persons, including the wives of the captain and the chief officer, were drowned.

Survivor's Narrative

Nelson gave the following account of the collision.

We left Antwerp on Friday morning for Port Talbot, in ballast. There were 18 or 19 crew on board, half the crew having been shipped at Antwerp. It was intended to ship the other half at Port Talbot. Captain Williams was accompanied by his wife, who lived in Anglesey, and Mrs Roberts, the chief officer's wife, was also on board. She belonged to Pwllheli. We were in tow of the tug *John Bull*, and all went well until about 4 o'clock this morning. We were off Pendeen, and I was wakened from my sleep by something banging into us.

I knew something had happened, and I rushed on deck. There I saw the lights of a steamer backing out. I rushed back to get some clothes, and then I went out on the poop, where I saw the captain and his wife, the chief officer and his wife and the third officer. The captain's wife shouted to the tug for help; the chief officer's wife was very calm. She was quite young. The *Kate Thomas* gradually heeled over. We were all hanging on for about eight minutes, but she gave one final plunge. I got a lifebuoy and sprang clear to try and save myself from being sucked down by the waves. Two or three huge seas enveloped me, and when I looked around there was nothing but a mass of foam, and the *Kate Thomas* had gone. Then I swam for the tug, and in a few minutes I saw the third officer in the water. I asked him if I could help him, and he replied 'No'. I then discovered he had his sea boots on, and I tried to take them off, but I could not manage it. He soon disappeared and I did not say anything when he went down. I then got to the tug and just managed to grasp a rope, by which I was hauled on board. I did not know what I was doing.

It is impossible for me to tell how the accident happened, but the captain of the tug told me the steamer steamed away and did not stop. I was in the water about 20 minutes. The tug cruised around for two hours, but we did not see any bodies. The crew was a mixed one. The captain's wife had made the round voyage, and after being home for a little holiday had returned to make another voyage. We all had our lights burning. It was a quarter of an hour before the *Kate Thomas* sank, but whether any efforts were made to launch the boats I do not know.

The name of the steamer which was in collision with the *Kate Thomas* was not known to Nelson or those on board the tug, but the steamship *India* put into Penzance yesterday and reported having been in collision off the Land's End. Lloyd's Agent at Penzance telegraphed yesterday: Steamer *India*, of Penzance, from Jersey for Weston Point, cargo china stone, has arrived here and reports having been in collision at about 4 am today with a ship, light, in tow, name unknown. *India* has considerable damage to bows.

According to another message, those on board the *India* were very reticent, but the captain said his ship came into collision with a sailing ship when about 25 miles north of Land's End between 3 and 4 am. Those on board *India* said they did not know the identity of the sailing ship, nor were they aware of its fate. The *India*'s bow bulwarks were stove in for five feet clean to the deck, but only one or two plates below were started, and these were above the water line. The *India* is only of 150 net tonnage. Her captain said he did not see any distress signal.

Tug Captain's Statement

The captain of the tug *John Bull* made a statement yesterday as to the disaster. He said that the steamer which came into collision with the barque first approached on the starboard within a quarter of a mile of the *Kate Thomas*. Then she came up on the port side and looked as if she would hit the tug. Whether she was attempting to go between the tug and the *Kate Thomas* he could not tell. There was a heavy sea running at the time, and he brought the tug around as quickly as possible. He thought the steamer would have rendered some assistance before the tug got around, but she steamed away.

The *Kate Thomas*, which had a net tonnage of 1,597, was built in 1885 by Messrs W Doxford & Sons, at Sunderland. She traded between English and Continental ports and South America with general cargo. She sailed mostly from Cardiff, not having been at Liverpool since 1907. It is considered doubtful whether any crew belonged to Liverpool, as only recently, when the vessel arrived at Antwerp, the crew were discharged at the end of the voyage, and new men were signed on. The third mate, named Spraymann, was an Antwerp man. The owners last evening received the following telegram from Falmouth:

Kate Thomas sunk this morning by unknown steamer whilst towing by tug. Suppose all excepting self lost.

Nelson, apprentice.

The Board of Trade Inquiry into the Loss of the *Kate Thomas* appears below:

Judgement was delivered in the Liverpool Police Buildings in the Board of Trade inquiry concerning the loss of the Liverpool barque *Kate Thomas* and 19 lives - the only survivor being an apprentice named John Joseph Nelson - after a collision off the Cornish coast with the steamer *India*.

The Court held that at the time of the collision the *Kate Thomas* and the tug *John Bull*, which was towing her, exhibited all the lights required by the regulations for preventing collisions at sea; and that the *Kate Thomas* kept her course and the speed required by the articles for preventing collisions at sea, but that proper measures were not taken by the *India* as required by the articles to keep out of the way of the *Kate Thomas*. The cause of the collision was the absence of an efficient look-out on the *India* and the improper use of the port helm of that vessel. The loss of life was caused by the *Kate Thomas* almost immediately heeling over to starboard, rapidly filling; and sinking within the space of ten minutes. Every possible effort was made by those on board the *John Bull* to render assistance, but no attempt to help was made by those on board the *India*, the reason alleged by them being that the latter vessel was herself seriously damaged. A good and proper look-out was not kept on the *India*. The Court found that the loss of the *Kate Thomas* was caused by the default of Thomas Frederick Mitchell, master of the *India*, in going below and leaving an able seaman named William John Stephens in charge of the deck, by the default of Stephens in not keeping a good and proper look out, and by Stephens ignorantly making improper use of the port helm of the *India*, thus bringing about a collision.

Neither the master nor the mate of the *India* held certificates of competency, and the Court was strongly of the opinion that for safe navigation those in charge of steam vessels of this description should be so certified.

Details of the *Kate Thomas*

She was a four-masted full-rigged iron ship built in 1885 by William Doxford & Sons, Sunderland (Official number: 91233). Dimensions: 258ft × 39ft 5ins × 23ft 1in, moulded draught 24ft 5in. The poop was 36ft and the forecastle 33ft. Tonnage 1748 GRT, 1693 NRT, and 1635 under deck tonnage. Built with one deck and two tiers of beams. Rigged with royals over single topgallants and double topsails. Launched in June 1885 at the shipyard of William Doxford & Sons, Sunderland, and delivered to the Kate Thomas Sailing Ship and Company, Liverpool. Managing owner was William Thomas and Company, Liverpool.

The Kate Thomas at the port of Caleta Coloso in Chile (courtesy of Tony Jones, Golau Llŷn Light)

Appendix XV

The *Eivion* Board of Trade Inquiry 1904

The Inquiry (No. 6752) into the Loss of the *Eivion* was issued in London by the Board of Trade on 9th day of December, 1904. A copy of the report is given below:

Finding and Order of a Naval Court held at the British Consulate-General at Valparaiso, on the 19th day of October, 1904, to investigate the circumstances attending the abandonment of the British sailing vessel *Eivion*, number 80229, of Caernarfon, on October 3rd, in latitude 54°S and 84°W longitude, owing to the cargo of coals being on fire.

The *Eivion* was a sailing vessel, barque-rigged, of 1,133 tons registered tonnage, official number 80229, built at Hylton, Durham in 1879 and belonging to the port of Caernarvon.

It appears from the evidence given before the Court that she sailed from Garston, Liverpool on June 14th last, bound for Tocopilla with a cargo of Blundell's Orell steam coal and a crew of 19 hands all told.

On September 10th, during heavy weather, a great sea washed away the lifeboat and gig. On September 30th at 4 pm, smoke was noticed coming through the chain pipes forward, and on opening the forehatches it was found to be full of smoke and the mean temperature of the three hatches was found to be 66°. Everything was battened down, including the ventilators. At midnight on October 1st the forehatches were blown overboard by an explosion and next morning October 2nd at 6.15 am the afterhatches were blown off. At 3 pm through the excessive rolling of the ship, the only remaining boat was staved in. An hour later a vessel was signalled which proved to be the *Lonsdale*, number 96382, of Liverpool. Rockets, blue lights, and a flare-up light on the gaff end were kept going until 11.30 pm when the *Lonsdale* rounded the lee of *Eivion* and promised to stand by until daylight. Wind and sea were increasing and the ship rolling badly. And with each heavy roll an explosion occurred throwing up a large quantity of coals. At about 6.30 am on October 3rd the *Lonsdale* in a very heavy sea launched her lifeboat, manned by Mr J O'Connor, first mate; C Larsen, carpenter; J Read, sailmaker; M Morrisson, AB and F Gradike, AB.

When this boat got alongside the *Eivion*, a big sea crashed her against the ship, staving in the boat and filling her with water. She returned to the *Lonsdale* with ten of the shipwrecked crew and returned to fetch the remainder – Captain Thomas and the two mates being the last to leave the ship. The *Eivion* was then sinking with all hatches off and dense clouds of smoke rising from each hatch, and was not under control. A fresh gale was blowing which shortly after increased to a howling gale of wind. The *Lonsdale* brought the crew of the *Eivion* to Valparaiso.

The Court, having regard to the circumstances above stated, finds as follows: That the master, Robert Thomas, appears to have navigated his vessel in a seamanlike and proper manner, and done everything in his power to save the ship and the lives of the crew.

That the mate, Mr E G Jones, and the second mate, Mr Charles Radcliffe, deserve praise for the manner in which they performed their duty. That the crew appear to have conducted themselves properly and done their utmost to save the ship.

The Court desires to place on record its high opinion of the able management and skilful navigation of Captain F K Fall, of the *Lonsdale*, and the gallant conduct of Mr J O'Connor, first mate; C Larsen, carpenter; J Read, sailmaker; M Morrisson,AB and F Gradike, AB, who volunteered to man the lifeboat, and by whose brave exertions the whole crew of the *Eivion* were saved.

The expenses of the Court, fixed at £4.13s, are approved.

Dated at Valparaiso this 19th day of October, 1904. Berry Cusack-Smith, HM's Consul-General for the Republic of Chile, President of Naval Court; Thom. Williams and John Jones – Members.

Appendix XVI

Index

The Criccieth Castle in Bristol Docks in the early twentieth century

Also from Delfryn Publications:

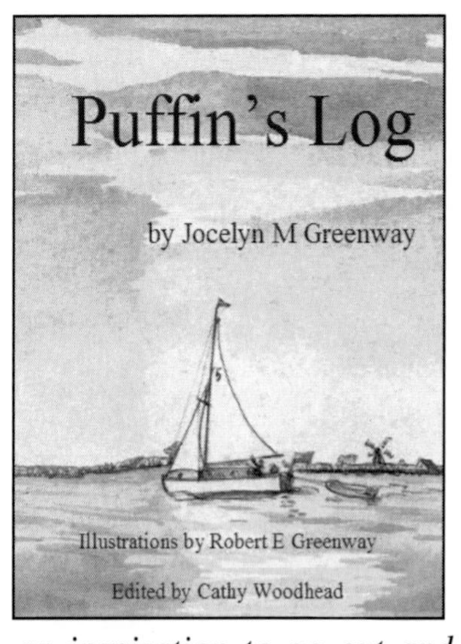

Puffin's Log (ISBN 978-0-9561469-0-8 May 2009) tells the story of the Greenway family's 1950s voyages in their 22-ft Hillyard sailing boat *Puffin,* from Jocelyn Greenway's articles with sketches, maps and photographs by her husband Robert. **Sir Chris Bonington** (Mountaineer) wrote of Puffin's Log:

'What a lovely and very special book. It's one that all generations can enjoy - the older, like myself, with nostalgia and the younger, as an inspiration to go out and adventure. I love the illustrations and the freshness of the narrative - it takes me back to my own childhood and the adventures that I enjoyed.'

A Sketchbook (ISBN 978-0-9561469-3-9 Dec 2009) is a selection of Robert Greenway's sketches. Robert and Jocelyn with their children shared many adventures around the world. Always accompanied with his paintbox and sketchpad Robert was prolific and this little book has line drawings and watercolour paintings from the 1950s to 1980 with scenes as far apart as Devon and Central Australia.